DATE DUE

JUL 24 2001			
Jul 24 01			

Young George Washington

YOUNG GEORGE WASHINGTON

 The Making of a Hero

JOHN ROSENBURG

The Millbrook Press • Brookfield, Connecticut

Photographs courtesy of The Mount Vernon Ladies' Association: p. 16; Library of Congress: pp. 20, 31, 35, 50, 87, 128, 145, 166-167; The Granger Collection, New York: pp. 25, 47, 154, 159; U.S. Army: p. 28; Yale University Library: p. 60; Corbis-Bettmann: p. 66; National Park Service: p. 113; Archives Nationales du Quebec: p. 118; National Archives of Canada: p. 163 (NMC-7782); Culver Pictures: p. 151; Maps by Joe LeMonnier.

Library of Congress Cataloging-in-Publication Data
Rosenburg, John M.
Young George Washington: the making of a hero / John Rosenburg.
p. cm.
Summary: A fictionalized biography, with emphasis on the early life, of the Virginia farmer's son who would eventually become a Revolutionary War leader and first President of the United States.
ISBN 0-7613-0043-0 (lib. bdg.)
1. Washington, George, 1732-1799—Childhood and youth—
Juvenile fiction. [1. Washington, George, 1732-1799—Childhood and youth—
Fiction. 2. United States—History—Colonial period, ca.1600-1775—Fiction.]
I. Title.
PZ7.R719185Yo   1997   [Fic]—DC21   96-21665   CIP   AC

Published by The Millbrook Press, Inc.
2 Old New Milford Road
Brookfield, Connecticut 06804

4

To the Howlands, Richardsons, Robinsons, Schillers, and Seaveys for years of encouragement and support.

Acknowledgments

It is George Washington himself to whom we are indebted for much of the basic information in the text of this book. Washington began keeping a diary at age sixteen, a practice he continued for years. Fortunately, most of his diaries have been found and preserved, allowing researchers to learn where he was and what he was doing and thinking for much of his daily life.

Washington's papers—letters, speeches, military orders, etc.—have also been preserved and can be found in books, articles, and library collections. Many of these, along with pertinent news stories, helped shape the manuscript.

Another diary that concerned Washington's role in the French and Indian War was written by Christopher Gist, who served as Washington's guide, scout, and Indian language interpreter.

Other extremely important sources of information include James Thomas Flexner's wonderful series of four books collectively titled *George Washington,* and Douglas Southall Freeman's monumental seven volumes of the same title.

Other sources include *George Washington: A Biography In His Own Words* from a series called "The Founding Fathers" edited by Ralph K. Andrist; *George Washington: 1732–1799* edited by Howard F. Bremer; *George Washington: The Image and the Man* by W. E. Woodward; and *The Oxford History of the American People* by Samuel Eliot Morrison.

I want to thank a considerate and patient trio who took the time to critique the manuscript and offer helpful suggestions: Joseph Seavey, Judith S. Richardson, and Sara Sheppard-Landis. Special thanks also go to Laura Walsh, my editor at The Millbrook Press, for her enthusiasm, encouragement, and cogent editorial advice.

Prologue

The message from King George II to the King's Council in Williamsburg, Virginia, was abundantly clear:

"If any Europeans who are not our subjects assemble in a hostile manner upon the River Ohio, intending by force of arms to erect certain forts within our territory, they are to be asked to peaceably depart," the King ordered. "And, if not withstanding your admonition, they still endeavor to carry out such unlawful and unjustifiable designs, we do strictly charge and command you to drive them out by force of arms."

The Council, called into emergency session by its president and chairman, Colonel William Fairfax, heard these words as it met in the ornate Governor's Palace on a rainy day in late October 1753 with the Royal Governor, the Honorable Robert Dinwiddie, in attendance.

It was Dinwiddie who sparked the King's outburst. That spring, he had written to London warning that the French were building a string of forts southward from their stronghold in Canada and edging northward from New Orleans, "clearly encroaching on English soil."

The French, he also pointed out, already occupied the St. Lawrence Valley, New Orleans, parts of Illinois, and several areas along the Great Lakes. In addition, Britain's archenemy at the time also claimed to own Louisiana, the Mississippi, and the Ohio and "all the land it drains."

British authorities vigorously disputed these claims. While well established in thirteen colonies along the Eastern Seaboard of North America, the British insisted that the rights to the Ohio Valley (then considered part of Virginia) belonged to the Crown as set forth in a cherished charter granted by King James I in 1609.

"Force of arms?" one Council member spluttered after Colonel Fairfax read the dispatch from His Royal Majesty.

"What did you expect?" asked Governor Dinwiddie, obviously annoyed.

"But that could mean . . ."

"Yes, it could," the Governor said grimly.

All were aware, of course, that Great Britain and France, two of the world's greatest military powers, were vigorously competing for commerce and territory in various parts of the world. But now, the Council members suddenly realized, the focal point of this struggle for supremacy had shifted to the Virginia frontier!

"Gentlemen!" Colonel Fairfax said, rapping for order in the midst of the general hubbub that ensued. "There's no need to speak of 'arms' just yet. First, we must, as the King has ordered, send a message to the French and ask them to leave our territory. If they do, fine. If they don't—well, we'll consider that problem when we face it."

"I agree," Governor Dinwiddie said. "And I'll get to work on a message to the French Commandant immediately."

"And when the message is prepared, what then?" a Council member asked.

"We have it delivered!" Dinwiddie blustered.

"Delivered?"

"Yes, delivered!"

"How?"

"By courier, of course!"

"I see," his questioner persisted. "So you envision a courier leaving here someday soon, then traveling hundreds of miles across the Alleghenies through a wilderness few white men have ever seen, let alone penetrated. And, assuming this courier can manage to pass through areas inhabited by hostile Indians, you expect him to be able to locate the French Commandant, hand him our invitation to leave our territory, and return here with the French reply?"

"Well, yes," Dinwiddie said. "That's the general idea."

"Impossible!" was the tart response.

"Gentlemen, His Majesty has spoken!" the Governor pleaded. "As his loyal subjects we must do our best to carry out his orders."

"I agree," a second councilman said. "But where will we find someone willing and able to undertake such a dangerous mission?"

After a brief silence during which all pondered this critical question, Colonel Fairfax thumped the table with his fist and said, "I know just the man!"

The "man" that Colonel Fairfax had in mind was a twenty-one-year-old Virginian named George Washington.

As Fairfax silently predicted, young Washington accepted the assignment. When he did so, he unwittingly launched the most important and influential military and political career in American history—a career highlighted by heartbreak, courage, defeat, adventure, treachery, suffering, victory, and one painful mistake after another.

This is the story of how that career began.

Young George Washington

$\mathcal{CO}$ As a poor, fatherless teenager, George Washington became more and more determined to be like his half-brother, Lawrence Washington, a tall, slender, blue-eyed man with a crop of curly, dark hair and long, mutton-chop sideburns, the fashion of the day.

And why not?

Lawrence was a war hero.

Lawrence had married beautiful Anne Fairfax, daughter of Colonel William Fairfax, one of the richest and most important men in Virginia.

Lawrence was a respected member of Virginia's House of Burgesses.

Lawrence owned a plantation on the Potomac River.

Lawrence was president of the Ohio Company, a land speculation company that owned 500,000 acres of land on the frontier.

Lawrence was Adjutant General of the Virginia militia, the colony's highest-ranking military officer.

Lawrence was a popular member of Virginia's elite in a two-class society — rich and poor.

Lawrence was also a close friend and business associate of Virginia's most important political figure, Governor Robert Dinwiddie.

Lawrence Washington was everything his younger half-brother George wished to be: handsome, charming, successful, heroic, and part of the Virginia elite. It was a lot for George to live up to.

Yes, he decided at a very early age, he wanted to be like Lawrence. If he succeeded, that meant he would be:

Well-mannered . . . successful . . . married . . . rich . . . and maybe even a military hero.

But, as is so often the case with those who dream heady dreams when they are young, there were major obstacles to overcome and thorny problems to solve.

⚬⚭B̲y the time he had reached his teens in 1745, young George Washington realized there were two things he must do if he ever hoped to emulate Lawrence, neither of which would be easy.

First and foremost, he must somehow educate himself.

His father, Augustine Washington, had first married Jane Butler, who died in 1730. That marriage produced two girls (one of whom died in infancy) and two boys, including Lawrence, who was fourteen years older than George.

Luckily for them, Lawrence and his brother, Augustine, Jr., were sent to school in England where, among other things, they learned how to become "gentlemen."

But after marrying Mary Ball in 1731, George's father no longer had the funds or inclination to send any more sons across the Atlantic Ocean for a formal education.

When Augustine Washington died, he left several tracts of land, a few cows and horses, and forty-nine slaves to his sons.

One tract, called Epsewasson, went to Lawrence, who renamed it Mount Vernon in honor of the British admiral he served under in Great Britain's war with Spain in 1740, when George was only eight.

Another tract, Wakefield — George's birthplace — went to Augustine, Jr., while a third tract, Ferry Farm, was to be George's when he turned twenty-one.

George was six when his father moved the family from Wakefield to Ferry Farm. The oldest of Mary Ball and Augustine Washington's five children, he was eleven when his father died.

Ferry Farm was a poor tract of land situated adjacent to a ferry crossing on the banks of the Rappahannock River. The farmhouse was a ramshackle, two-story structure with four rooms on the ground floor and two above. It was so small that three beds had to be set up in the parlor to accommodate part of the family. And it was so ill-equipped that there were barely enough eating utensils and dishes to go around.

There is evidence that George attended school from age eleven to fourteen and that he had a tutor whenever one was available in his part of the country.

And since some of his copybooks have been preserved, it is clear that he relied heavily on another important source of educational information: books.

$\mathcal{O}\!\!\mathcal{D}$ **B**ooks were rare in Colonial Virginia. But, somehow, George found two that he felt sure would help him improve himself.

One was titled *Rules of Civility and Decent Behavior in Company and Conversation.* Before passing the book on, he carefully copied all 110 of the "rules" and tried to memorize them. Among them were these:

> When face to face with others, do not cough, sneeze or yawn.
> When others are present, never remove your trousers.
> When others are present, never pluck your head and kill fleas, lice or ticks.

Other rules advised him to avoid talking while his mouth was full of food; to avoid making noise while eating; to respect the elderly; to make worthwhile friends; to keep his clothes neat; and to always wear a smile.

The second book, *The Young Man's Best Companion,* also contained advice on behavior. But, to George, it was important in another way; it was filled with facts and fascinating "how-to" hints.

The *Companion* described, for example, how lumber and land could be measured; how legal documents and letters should be written; how trees should be planted; and how interest on sums of money should be calculated.

Determined to be accepted in polite company, Washington copied and memorized the accepted "rules" of behavior popular in his day. One of the most important was "Never clean your teeth on the tablecloth."

Luckily, young Washington liked math and was good with numbers. He learned, through hard study, all sorts of practical things, such as the tables of weights and measurements.

More important, he also learned some advanced math — enough to enable him to make rough surveys of land.

Books, George realized, were very important. But he knew he could not possibly achieve his goal of becoming another Lawrence as long as he remained tied to Ferry Farm. For at this stage of his life he could barely write a coherent letter. His spelling was awful and his grammar atrocious. Even his speech was awkward.

In letters and on occasional visits to Mount Vernon, he complained about his situation to Lawrence, always a sympathetic listener. But the more he growled about it to his mother, a large, gaunt woman with pulled-back gray hair, a pinched nose, and a thin, small mouth, the more adamant she became.

"I need you here and you're going to stay put!" his mother declared whenever he even hinted at leaving.

Over and over again, however, he told himself, "I've got to get away from here!"

But like many teenagers brimming with good health and ambition, young Washington was confronted with two basic questions: "Where do I go?" "How do I support myself?" (Especially without skills!)

Suddenly, life—once so bleak and unpromising—offered a ray of hope. A stranger passing Ferry Farm on his way south handed George a note. (In Colonial times, this is how mail was often delivered.) The note read:

> Col. Fairfax will be stopping at Boar's Head Inn, F'cksburg, on way to Wils'burg Wed's-day next. Don't tell yr mother, but meet Col. before noon that day.
>
> Yr loving bro, Lawrence.

The wealthy former army Colonel and the teenage farm boy were in sharp contrast to one another when they met that warm spring day in Fredricksburg.

Fairfax was a short, pudgy man in his mid-fifties with white hair and a neatly trimmed white goatee. Elegantly dressed as always, he was attended by a manservant, a coachman, and a footman.

The fourteen-year-old Washington, on the other hand, wore a floppy, shapeless hat and the rough garb of a typical farmhand. Gangly and awkward, he was also taller and generally bigger than the older man. And since he had sculled up the river from Ferry Farm in a small, leaky, flat-bottomed boat, his feet were muddy.

But these differences in age and appearance

didn't seem to bother the pair as they sat down in the Colonel's rooms to talk.

"Does your mother know you've come to meet me?" the Colonel asked.

Washington's answer was a simple "No."

"Good," the Colonel said with a smile.

Fairfax then handed the boy a letter. "This is from Lawrence," he said, suddenly becoming serious. "You're to open it and read it carefully. And when you are finished, I will ask you a question and you will have to give me an honest answer. Understand?"

Young Washington, more puzzled than ever, could only nod.

"Dear George," Lawrence wrote, "if you wish, you may have a career in the British Navy. All you need to do is to sign on as a midshipman under Captain Green, a friend of mine who is in command of a British vessel now in Virginia waters. Please convey your decision to Colonel Fairfax. If the answer is 'yes' he will give you further instructions. If you decline, just forget all about this proposal."

"Well, lad," Colonel Fairfax said after Washington had read the letter, "do you think you want to become a Navy man and sail the seven seas?"

Without a second thought, Washington exclaimed, "Yes! Oh, yes sir!"

"Well, in that case, I have another letter here

that you are to give to your mother," Colonel Fairfax said. "If you were not interested in serving under Captain Green, I would have torn both letters up, as your mother doesn't take kindly to anyone interfering in her affairs. But, since you have decided affirmatively, Lawrence and I believe your mother will recognize that this is a grand opportunity for you and will favor it."

Thankfully for the course of American history, the Colonel and Lawrence were wrong.

Mary Washington took several weeks to make a decision regarding Lawrence's proposal to George. During this period, she consulted her friends and also wrote to her brother, Joseph Ball, in London.

Ball was totally opposed to Lawrence's proposal. He said in a scathing reply to Mary that his nephew "had better be put apprentice to a tinker. The Royal Navy will cut him, slash him, and use him like a Negro, or, rather, like a dog."

Young Washington, he added, should "stick to farming," for if he worked hard he would "live more comfortably, and leave his family in better bread" than even a Captain of a British ship.

When George heard this, he cried out in protest. "Uncle Joe is wrong! And Lawrence is right!"

Reluctantly, Mary Ball Washington gave her son permission to join the British Royal Navy. But luckily, she changed her mind at the last minute.

After much turmoil at Ferry Farm, Mary suddenly gave in.

"Go ahead," she said one night, "join the Navy. But I warn you . . . ."

The warning fell on deaf ears. George packed his bags immediately.

The next morning, however, Mary changed her mind. "You can unpack," she said grimly. "You're not going."

COMary's decision so angered Lawrence Washington that he made a trip to Ferry Farm to confront her.

She received her elegant, suave, and handsome visitor cordially enough. But when Lawrence touched on George's future, she grew surly, repeating her old refrain.

"I appreciate your interest in my son, Mr. Washington, but I need him here," she said when George was out of hearing. "There's the animals, the other children, and the land to be taken care of. I can't do it all by myself."

"No, of course not," Lawrence soothed. "But if you won't let him join the Navy, surely you'll let him visit Anne and me more often and stay longer."

"Why? Why should he do that? Being around you and your friends and them Fairfaxes will only give him big ideas. And later he'll be sorry!"

"He's a very unusual boy, Mary," Lawrence argued. "Intelligent. Ambitious. And he can be quite charming at times."

"Charming? Charming don't put food on the table."

In the end, it was Lawrence's charm (and persistence) that finally persuaded Mary to loosen her apron strings. When she did so, young Washington entered an exciting new world.

Instead of existing close to poverty on a crowded, run-down farm, George found himself in a stylish and roomier home and projected into a life of fox hunts and parties, good and abundant food, and fine clothes.

But there was something else: He went to school. He took dancing lessons. And then there was Belvoir.

Upriver only four miles, the elegant Fairfax plantation was a constant center of social activity for members of Virginia's wealthiest and most important families, with many members his own age. With these newly found friends, he hunted, fished, played games and—for the first time in his life—attended concerts and plays.

In fact, when *Cato,* a play about an enemy of Julius Caesar, was staged at Belvoir, George played the role of Juba, Cato's adopted son who falls in love with Cato's daughter.

He was so impressed by many of the lines in the play that he copied them, including these:

A Roman soul is bent on higher views;
To civilize the rude, unpolish'd world,
And lay it under the restraint of laws;

It was at Belvoir, the home of the Fairfaxes, that young Washington discovered music and drama, and became closely associated with one of the most prominent families in all of Virginia.

To make man mild and sociable to man,
To cultivate the wild, licentious, save
With wisdom, discipline and liberal arts,
The embellishment of life. Virtues like these
Make human nature shine, reform the soul,
And break our fierce barbarians into men.

Did the high moral tone of these lines have any effect on Washington's future conduct? It may be argued that they did. But no one will ever know for sure.

$\mathcal{O}\!\!\mathcal{E}$ F̲ew names in Colonial Virginia were more prominent than "Fairfax."

Colonel Fairfax, for example, was not only President of Virginia's influential King's Council but was also a major stockholder in the Ohio Company along with Lawrence and Governor Dinwiddie.

More important, as young Washington and many other Virginians knew, the Fairfax name was linked to British royalty.

The family connection began with John Culpeper of Wigsell, Kent, in the 1640s. For some reason lost in history, King Charles I favored Culpeper and bestowed upon him the title of "Baron."

Culpeper's ties to Charles I and subsequently to Charles II brought him something else: The rights to five million acres of land "bounded and within the heads" of Virginia's Potomac and Rappahannock rivers, a tract larger than the state of New Jersey.

The land passed to the Fairfax family when Culpeper's daughter married Thomas, fifth Lord Fairfax, in 1690. On his death, the land went to the next Lord Fairfax.

To manage his property, the sixth Lord Fairfax called on his cousin William, whose motto was "I trust in God I shall never procure the disesteem of any relation."

After serving in the military and representing the Crown in various posts along the western rim of the British Empire, Colonel Fairfax, accompanied by his second wife and six children, moved to Virginia in the mid-1730s to take up his new duties as Lord Fairfax's representative.

Shortly after his arrival, he built Belvoir. The handsome brick mansion, situated on the south slope of the Potomac, was Virginia's finest. In addition to several bedrooms, it contained two parlors, a ballroom, and a large library.

Two more members of the Fairfax family soon arrived at Belvoir—one in 1746, the other a year later. The first was the Colonel's oldest child, George William. The second—who would soon play a major role in young Washington's development—was Lord Fairfax of Cameron, the richest and most important Fairfax of all!

Thin of face, slight of build, but aristocratic and learned, George William Fairfax returned to Belvoir when he was twenty-one, having completed a long stint abroad at English schools.

Despite the seven-year difference in their ages, and the sharp contrast in their backgrounds and physical appearance, George William and young Washington soon became fast friends.

The slightly eccentric Thomas Lord Fairfax of Cameron came to Belvoir in 1747 and brought a dramatic change to Washington's life by inviting George to survey his vast holding of wilderness land.

Lord Fairfax of Cameron, on the other hand, was a smallish man in his mid-fifties and somewhat eccentric; he had a passion for clothes and fox hunting and hated women. (It was said he had once been jilted and never got over it.)

Since young Washington loved fox hunting and was a superb horseman, he and His Lordship got along famously.

On returning from a hunt that winter with George William and young Washington, His Lordship suddenly switched the topic of conversation from horses, hounds, and foxes to another subject.

"I say, lads, I assume you know I have a bit of property here about, what?" His Lordship began.

The boys nodded.

"Yes, of course," he went on. "And one must protect his rights to property. Rightly so, eh?"

The boys nodded again, wondering where this one-sided conversation was going.

"Yes, of course. And so I've made a decision. Can you guess what it is? Eh? What?"

"No, M'Lord," William said as he and an amused young Washington exchanged glances.

"Yes, well, I'm going to have every acre of my land surveyed, marked, and recorded," His Lordship said. "That way there will never be a dispute about who owns what. Intelligent thing to do, what?"

"Yes, M'Lord," George William said.

"Glad you agree," His Lordship went on. "Now then, I have already contacted James Genn, the surveyor for Prince William Township. He's going to divide my property into lots, each large enough for a farm.

"And you, George William, you are to go along as my representative. And you, George Washington, you are to help Genn and be a companion to George William. What say you, eh? What?"

Thrilled by the prospect of a great adventure, both joyously accepted.

"It's settled, then," His Lordship chuckled, proud of his decision.

For fifteen-year-old George Washington, the trip would mark another major turning point in his life.

Fryday the 11th of March 1747/8.
A Journal of my Journey over the Mountains . . . .

Thus began a diary (based on an old-style calendar used in Britain) written by young Washington as the surveying party was about to leave that spring.

Washington decided to keep a record of all he was about to experience so he would never forget what it was like to go into the vast wilderness west of Mount Vernon and Ferry Farm.

It was, he knew, a mysterious and dangerous country, the only inhabitants being wild animals, a few white men, and several Indian tribes, some of them hostile.

The diary he purchased was actually *Virginia's Almanac,* an annual publication with many blank pages. It measured only four by six inches and easily fit into a pocket of his trousers or jacket.

Along with his faulty spelling and grammar, Young Washington started the first of many entries this way: "Began my journey in company with George Fairfax, Esqr.: We traveled this day 40 miles to Mr. George Neavels in Prince William County."

Early the following morning, they were joined by the surveyor, James Genn, and several woodsmen. After becoming acquainted, the group, with Genn leading, headed their horses west toward the Blue Ridge Mountains. By nightfall, they had reached the cabin of Captain John Ashby on the Shenandoah River.

On Sunday, March 13, young Washington wrote in his diary: "Rode to Lordships Quarter about 4 miles higher up the River. We went through the most beautiful Groves of Sugar Trees & spent the best part of the Day in admiring the Trees & richness of the land."

On March 16, after surveying from dawn to dark, the group made its way to Captain Isaac Pennington's, where young Washington learned an important lesson about life in a log cabin on the frontier.

THE
VIRGINIA
ALMANACK
FOR THE
Year of our LORD GOD 1765.
BEING THE FIRST AFTER
BISSEXTILE, or LEAP-YEAR.

WHEREIN ARE CONTAINED

The LUNATIONS, CONJUNCTIONS, ECLIPSES, the SUN and MOON's Rising and Setting, WEATHER, &c. Calculated according to ART, and referred to the HORIZON of 30 Degrees North Latitude, and a Meridian of Five Hours West from the City of *London:* Fitting VIRGINIA, MARYLAND, N. CAROLINA, &c. Also a Table of COURT DAYS, Description of the ROADS through the Continent, a List of the COUNCIL and HOUSE of BURGESSES of VIRGINIA, with the most approved Treatise extant upon HEMP, in which is the whole Process of getting that valuable Commodity ready for Exportation, &c.

TO WHICH IS ADDED,

A Collection of approved MAXIMS, entertaining EPIGRAMS, curious ANECDOTES, diverting STORIES, &c. &c. Calculated for Instruction and Amusement.

By T H E O P H I L U S W R E G, *Philom.*

Thefe TWO *fure* THINGS *we always have in* VIEW, *To benefit* OURSELVES, *and pleafure* YOU.

W I L L I A M S B U R G:
Printed and Sold by JOSEPH ROYLE, and C°.

While on the surveying expedition, Washington kept his first of many diaries in the blank pages of The Virginia Almanac. *He recorded many events, including his narrow escape from a straw mattress set ablaze by the campfire.*

[35]

"We got our suppers," he noted, "& was Lighted into a Room & I not being so good a woodsman as the rest of my Company I striped myself very orderly & went into the Bed as they called it when to my Surprize I found it to be nothing but a Little Straw Matted together without sheets or anything else but a Thread Bear blanket with double its Weight of Vermin such as Lice & Fleas . . . ."

The group spent the next night in a small settlement named Frederick Town, where he cleaned himself thoroughly "to get ride of the game we ketched the night before . . ." and slept in a good feather bed "with clean sheets which was a very agreeable regale . . . ."

Heavy rains and swollen rivers halted progress over the next several days. On March 23, however, at about two o'clock in the afternoon, there was an interruption of another sort: The surveyors came face-to-face with a band of about thirty Indians.

The Indians, Washington wrote, "were coming from war" but "with only one scalp."

To lift their spirits, Genn gave the Indians some liquor. This, said Washington, "put them in the Humour of Dauncing . . ." and soon the Indians staged a war dance for their newfound "friends."

In the longest entry, Washington described the dance in this way:

They clear a large circle & make a great fire in the Middle then seats themselves around it then the Speaker makes a grand Speech & tells them in what Manner they are to Daunce. After he has finished the best Dauncer jumps up as one awakened out from a Sleep & runs and Jumps about the Ring in a most comicle Manner. He is followed by the Rest then begins there Musicians to Play. The music is a Pot half (full) of Water with a Deerskin Stretched over it as tight as it can and a Goard with Shott in it to Rattle & a Piece of Horses tail tied to it to make it look fine. The one keeps Rattling and the other Drumming all the While the other is Dauncing.

Other entries in the diary spoke of:

★ Encountering "rattled" snakes, storms and difficult river crossings
★ Dining with a Justice of the Peace without a tablecloth or knife to eat with but, "as good luck would have it we had knives of our own "
★ Shooting wild turkeys
★ Each member of the party being "his own cook. Our spits was forked sticks. Our Plates was a Large Chip [of wood]. As for Dishes we had none."

The final entry in this diary (one of many that Washington kept throughout his lifetime) read:

"Wednesday the 13th of April 1748, Mr. Fairfax got safe home and I myself safe to my Brothers which concludes my Journal."

He was only sixteen, but suddenly he knew where he was headed.

He would become a surveyor. The thirty-three days he spent with James Genn convinced him that surveying was a highly regarded and valued profession. And, significantly, among the highest paid!

As a surveyor, he could at last begin to reach the objective closest to his heart: becoming the kind of man personified by Lawrence.

Spurred on by dreams and determination, he reached his first goal on July 20, 1749, when he became the official surveyor for Culpeper County.

Two days later—and only fifteen months after his travels with Genn—he surveyed four hundred acres for Richard Barnes. His reward? Cash to the tune of more than two pounds! (Approximately equal to three dollars—a good sum in 1749.)

That same summer, he also landed a job as assistant to a surveyor who was to lay out a new town at the head of the Potomac. The town was named Alexandria (and remains so to this day).

In the fall, he returned to the mountains alone to mark out more lots for Lord Fairfax and others. It was not an easy life, as he was often without food and adequate shelter.

Occasionally, after a long day, he would come

upon the cabin of a trader or trapper and be invited to dinner and to spend the night.

In a letter to a friend, which showed no improvement in composition, he said he would often lay fully clothed before the hearth ". . . upon a Little Hay . . . or Bairskin which ever is to be had with Man Wife and Children like a Parcel of Dogs or Catts & happy is he that gets the Birth nearest the fire . . . ."

But one thing made it all worthwhile: the pay.

"A doubbleloon," he boasted, "is my constant gain every Day that the Weather will permit . . . some times Six Pistoles . . ." (A doubloon has been valued at $7.20, a pistole at about half that amount.)

Hoping to soon join the social circle that included Lawrence and the Fairfaxes, he worked very hard and carefully saved his earnings.

While he invested most of his savings in land, he also used some of his hard-earned cash to order several items of expensive new clothing from London. For now his attention had turned to something else: girls.

Not long after his arrival in Virginia, Lord Fairfax built a hunting lodge for himself across the Blue Ridge. He called it Greenway Court.

Young Washington often stayed at Greenway while surveying His Lordship's property in the area. And during the evenings, after a long day in the woods and fields, he would often play cards and other games with His Lordship and guests.

He would also write long letters (still ungrammatical but growing in eloquence) to his closest friends and relatives. The exchange of personal letters, he said repeatedly, represented "the greatest mark of friendship and esteem."

While writing letters gave him a chance to discuss his experiences in the forest, they also presented an outlet for something else: personal secrets.

One night at Greenway, for instance, he said in a letter to a cousin:

> . . . a very agreeable young lady lives in the same house [where] I might was my heart disengaged [from someone else] pass my time very pleasantly . . . .
>
> [But, he added,] thats only adding Fuel to the fire [and] it makes me the more uneasy for by often and unavoidably being in Company with her revives my former Passion for a young Low Land Beauty whereas was I to live more retired from young Women I might in some measure eliviate my sorrows by burying that chast(e) and troublesome Passion in the grave of oblivion and enternall forgetfullness for as I am very well asured that's the

only antidote or remedy that I ever shall be re-
leived by or only recess that can administer
any cure or help to me as I am well convinced
was I ever to attempt anything I should only
get a denial which would only be adding grief
to uneasiness.

Later, in an attempt to bury his "troublesome Passion," he wrote this poem to a Virginia belle
named Frances Alexander:

From your bright sparkling Eyes, I was undone;
Rays, you have more transparent than the sun,
A midst its glory in the rising Day,
None can you equal in your bright array;
Constant in your calm and unspotted mind;
Equal to all, but will to none Prove kind,
So Knowing, seldom one so Young, and you'l Find.
Ah! woe's me, that I should love and conceal,
Long have I wish'd, but never dare reveal,
Even though severly Loves Pains I feel;
Xerxes that great, wasn't free from Cupid's Dart,
And all the greatest Heroes, felt the smart.

Suddenly, young Washington's reveries about his
"passion" and "Cupid's dart" were rudely interrupted by grim news from Mount Vernon: Lawrence was seriously ill.

⚬⚭H̲e made another trip across
the Blue Ridge during the summer of 1750.
   This one had nothing to do with surveying.

This one, it was hoped, would save Lawrence's life.

During the previous fall (1749), Lawrence, Anne, and George William Fairfax and his new wife, Sarah "Sally" Cary Fairfax, had gone to the Governor's Ball in Williamsburg, a colorful annual affair. When Lawrence returned to Mount Vernon, he was coughing heavily.

Lawrence had tuberculosis, a disease contracted while he was with a Virginia regiment serving under Admiral Edward Vernon in South America during the war with Spain. (At the time, it was an untreatable and usually fatal disease.)

"George," he said one night after a severe coughing spell, "have you ever heard of warm springs in the mountains that help the sick?"

"Yes," Washington said. "We found them when I was with Genn. The Indians and others say that bathing in the springs cures many ailments. I know I can find them again, if you want to go."

"I'll go anywhere to get rid of this cough."

With George taking the lead, the brothers rode up and over the Blue Ridge to where the mineral springs were located (now Berkeley Springs, West Virginia).

After bathing in the warm waters several times, Lawrence seemed to improve. After another trip to the springs the following year, however, he was much worse.

"Maybe we should take a trip to Barbados," young Washington suggested. "The tropical air might help you."

"I don't think anything can help me," a dispirited Lawrence said.

"You won't know unless you try," Washington urged. "I'll go with you."

After a little more coaxing, Lawrence relented.

During the voyage (his first and only one beyond America's shores), young Washington kept another diary. In this one, he wrote excitedly about sightings of sharks, dolphins, and barracudas and the fury of a major storm.

Once on the island, the brothers were relieved and delighted to be told by a doctor that Lawrence could be cured. This welcome news prompted them to accept several invitations to dinner.

Lawrence, however, grew steadily worse. At the same time, George was stricken with smallpox. By the time he recovered, the disease had lightly scarred his nose. (In the future, he would be immune to further infection from what was then a ruthless killer.)

In early December, Lawrence's cough became almost unbearable. He blamed it on the damp, intense heat of the island.

Desperate for relief, Lawrence decided to sail to the drier climate of Bermuda.

"But you must go home," Lawrence told George. "You can't help me. And someone must look after Anne and Mount Vernon."

Reluctantly, George agreed.

Five months later, Lawrence wrote: "The unhappy state of health which I labor under, makes me uncertain as to my return. If I grow worse, I shall hurry home to my grave."

Lawrence soon returned to Mount Vernon. He died there on July 26, 1752, at the age of thirty-four.

He was sixteen. She was eighteen. He was poor relations. She was upper-class.

He was an overgrown puppy, awkward and eager, and tongue-tied around women.

She was tall, sophisticated, dark-eyed, attractive, vivacious, and flirtatious.

She was Sally Fairfax, the wife of George William, his best friend.

Still, from the moment Washington first laid eyes on Sally, he knew what it was like to be truly in love.

He was never sure how she felt about him. But of course, he realized that they would never have a future together.

And so, when he was twenty and the owner of almost 1,500 acres of land, he turned his attention and charms on someone else, Elizabeth "Betsy" Fauntleroy. She was fifteen and the daughter of a prominent Virginia family.

After a brief courtship, he proposed marriage. She promptly turned him down. Undaunted, he wrote to her father, enclosing a second proposal to Betsy.

In his letter to Betsy's father he said that he was very ill, but when he recovered he would "wait on Miss Betsy, in hopes of a Revocation of the former, cruel sentence, and see if I can meet with any alteration in my favor . . . ."

Betsy's answer? She married someone else.

Washington had never worn a military uniform. He had never seen a major military fortification. He had never commanded or drilled a military unit. And he was almost totally unfamiliar with both the strategy and weapons of war.

Still, he yearned to be a military officer. And the post he wanted—and for which he vigorously campaigned—was that of Adjutant General of the Virginia militia (roughly equivalent to the present-day National Guard). Significantly, this was the command that Lawrence had held until his death.

The House of Burgesses, however, decided to divide the colony into four districts, each with its own military unit.

Undiscouraged by this change, Washington continued his campaign. Finally, he got his wish.

On November 6, 1752—less than four months after Lawrence died—he accepted his appointment as commander of the smallest of the new military districts. His rank was that of Major; the pay, one hundred pounds per year.

Two months later, Anne Fairfax Washington married George Lee of Staunton in Westmoreland County. With the only child born of her marriage to Lawrence, she moved in with her new husband and leased Mount Vernon to Washington.

Now, as he approached his twenty-first birthday, it seemed as though he would be able to settle back into the life of a country squire who, in his spare time, would carry out the mostly ceremonial duties of a local military commander.

But he was wrong. For that October (1753), Colonel Fairfax paid him a visit at Mount Vernon. During a long meeting, the Colonel reviewed the dangerous situation brewing on the western frontier.

"The French," he said, "are encroaching on our territory, and His Majesty wants us to take steps to stop them. If we move quickly and warn them off, we may avert a war."

"But the French may ignore us," Washington said.

After Lawrence's widow moved to the home of her new husband, she leased Mount Vernon to twenty-one-year-old Washington for the price of twenty pounds of tobacco a year.

"True. But we must try."

Washington thought a moment, then said, "So the Governor wants me to deliver the warning?"

Colonel Fairfax drew a deep breath. "Will you?" he asked.

"I'll try," Washington said.

After shaking hands with Washington, Colonel Fairfax left for Belvoir, a relieved and happy man.

earing his first military uniform, designed and fitted only a few months earlier, Major Washington left the Governor's Palace and rode north through Williamsburg on October 31, 1753, with Dinwiddie's orders, the letter to the French, and a fresh diary tucked in his saddlebags.

In a rugged sort of way, he had grown into a handsome man. He had blue-gray eyes, a prominent nose and cheekbones, and a thick mop of reddish hair. He was also solidly built, with unusually long legs and arms and big hands and feet.

Always an imposing figure, he sat upon his horse with extraordinary grace and ease as it danced this way and that through the crowded streets of the town. Even under ordinary circumstances, his unusual size, obvious strength, and remarkable horsemanship would turn heads. But as he moved along on this day, there were whispers, loud comments, and even an occasional hoot of derision.

For, by now, almost all of Virginia knew where he was going and why. And varied opinions on the success or failure of this unprecedented and potentially explosive mission were openly and vigorously aired.

But Major Washington, who was not given much to speaking about himself or his activities, paid little attention to all the talk that was swirling around him.

Still, he must have realized that he faced a formidable task. After all, he could not speak French and knew virtually nothing of French culture and manners. And although he was somewhat familiar with the ways of Indians, he had never mastered the language of any of the many tribes he had encountered in the nearby forests. Nevertheless, as requested by Dinwiddie, he was to:

★ Travel hundreds of miles over a northwesterly route that would cross the dangerous mountains and rivers of both the Blue Ridge and the mighty Alleghenies

★ Contact various Indian chiefs known to be friendly to Britain and learn where the French could be found

★ Persuade the Indians to provide him with an escort so that he could reach the French and return safely

★ Present Dinwiddie's letter to the highest-ranking French officer ". . . in the name of his Britannic Majesty and demand an answer thereto "

The letter, polite but firm, noted that "the lands upon the River Ohio in the Western Parts of the Colony of Virginia are so notoriously known to be the Property of the Crown of Great Britain, that it is a matter of equal Concern and Surprise to me to hear that a body of French

Governor Robert Dinwiddie of Virginia was the author of the polite but firm message directed at the French occupying the Ohio River Valley, an area that was considered British soil.

Forces are erecting Fortresses and making Settlements upon the River within his Majesty's dominions . . . ."

The letter went on to ask the French to leave the Ohio.

Washington's orders, on the other hand, made it clear that he was to be more than a messenger.

"You are to diligently inquire into the number and force of the French on the Ohio, and the adjacent country," his orders read, "how they are likely to be assisted from Canada; and what are the difficulties and conveniences of that communication, and the time required for it.

". . . and to be truly informed what forts the French have erected, and where; how they are garrisoned and appointed; and what is their distance from each other . . . and from the best intelligence you can procure, you are to learn what gave occasion to this expedition of the French; how they are likely to be supported and what their pretensions are . . . ."

In other words, he was also to be a spy.

Since Washington's first stop would be in Fredericksburg, he had no choice but to visit his mother. As expected, however, the visit to Ferry Farm proved to be a painful ordeal.

"And now, you come here for an hour or two and you're off again!" she complained, sweeping a strand of gray hair out of her face. "Why?"

"Because I have to get back before winter sets in and there is no time to lose," he answered quietly, stifling his displeasure.

"You said all that before. But why you? Why must you do Dinwiddie's bidding?"

"There are several reasons."

"And the most important is that Dinwiddie, Fairfax, and their friends have a sizable investment in the Ohio Company, which just happens to own a lot of land out there," she flared. "That's it, isn't it?"

"No!" Washington snapped, angry now.

"Then it must be 'honor,' 'duty,' or some such silly thing."

Washington took a deep breath and tried to answer in an even tone. "That's part of it. But mostly, it's because I have an obligation to the Fairfax family."

" 'The Fairfax family'," she mocked. "What about your obligation to me?"

Since this was an old argument that never seemed to end, Washington cut his visit short.

Leaving the house, he led his horse aboard the rickety ferry moored nearby and crossed the slow-moving Rappahannock to the far side, where he mounted and rode on to Fredricksburg.

Once in town, he sought out a man named Jacob van Braam. With Dinwiddie's prior approval, he offered van Braam, who spoke French, a job as an interpreter.

Van Braam, a tall, lean man in his mid-thirties with a large nose and ears, usually enjoyed adventure, as did many of his Dutch countrymen. Still, he hesitated.

"Surely I'd like to go with you, George," he said plaintively, "but me translation is na' so good."

"It's better than no translation at all," Washington pointed out. "Besides, I'm told I can trust you and rely on you if we run into difficulty."

Hearing those words, van Braam promptly agreed to join Washington in the attempt to locate and deal with the French.

The next morning, with his uniform packed carefully into his saddlebags, Washington led the way out of Fredricksburg. Two weeks later, after crossing the Blue Ridge and the Shenandoah Valley, the two men reached Wills Creek (now Cumberland, Maryland), a small settlement on the eastern slope of the Alleghenies.

On their arrival, Washington looked up Christopher Gist, a short, wiry, weatherbeaten man in his middle forties who was often employed by the Ohio Company. Colonel Fairfax had recommended Gist as an experienced woodsman who knew all about Indian ways and customs and could speak several tribal languages.

When Washington explained what he hoped to do and asked whether Gist was willing to join his party, the frontiersman raked the young Major up and down with a pair of sharp blue eyes, stroked his thick black beard for a moment, then uttered one word.

"Yup," he said.

At Wills Creek, Washington also engaged four

other men—all of them white traders and trappers—and bought several pack horses, loading them with enough provisions to last a month.

It was a promising start to a difficult undertaking, but only a start.

$\mathcal{C\hspace{-2pt}O}$Heavy rains and snow slowed the party considerably as it moved westward to its next destination, the cabin of trader John Frazier, a British subject.

The cabin, situated at the confluence of the Monongahela River and Turtle Creek, was much larger than those usually found on the frontier.

A huge fireplace dominated the wall opposite the central entranceway. To the left were crude wooden benches and chairs, a large dining table, a pantry, and an area that served as a kitchen.

To the right was a long counter that bore the weight of scores of animal skins, among them fox, wolf, muskrat, otter, and beaver. And crowded together on the wall behind the counter were dozens more, mounted on stretchers to help them dry.

To the right of the fireplace, a ladder led to a loft where rough beds, filled with straw, were scattered about the floor.

Ignoring the rancid odor of the pelts, Washington's group settled down to a dinner of venison stew on the night of its arrival. And during the course of the dinner, Frazier confirmed what the King's Council feared: The French had, indeed, built several forts along the Ohio to the north.

"And our Indians ain't too happy about it, either," Frazier said.

"What about the Forks?" Washington asked, referring to the area to the northwest where the Monongahela joined the Allegheny to form the Ohio (which, to the Indians, meant "Beautiful River").

"They had a work force there, but their commander—General Marin, I think it was—died and they went into winter quarters."

"Do you know where?"

"I'm not sure, but I think it's Le Boeuf, farther north," Frazier said.

"Then nothing was built at the Forks?" Washington asked.

"That's what my Indians tell me, but you never know."

From a briefing given by Dinwiddie, Washington knew that the Ohio Company and the Crown hoped to be the first to build on the Forks (now Pittsburgh). If successful, Britain would then occupy the most important military position in that part of the country.

As the dinner wore on, Washington made it clear that he was anxious to move ahead.

"Don't be in a hurry," Frazier warned. "The rivers are flooding and can't be forded, for one thing. And . . . ."

"And?" Washington prodded.

"And three tribes of Indians friendly to the French are on the warpath."

"Why?" Washington asked.

"They know you're coming," Frazier said darkly.

Washington was in no mood to wait for the waters of the Monongahela to recede. Nor was he inhibited by the chilling news that Indians sympathetic to the French were thirsting for British blood.

After borrowing a canoe from Frazier the next morning, Washington, Gist, and van Braam paddled hurriedly northward toward the Forks, leaving the rest of his party to make the trip overland.

To his relief, he saw no sign of life at the Forks, nor any evidence of construction.

Disembarking on a strip of land that separated the two rivers until they formed the Ohio, he and his two companions made a careful inspection of the area.

Later, after setting up camp, he jotted down his impressions in his diary.

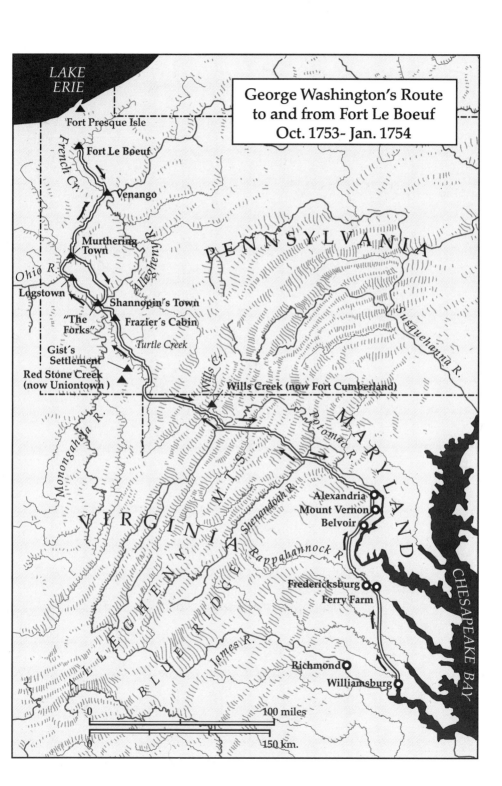

LAKE
ERIE

George Washington's Route
to and from Fort Le Boeuf
Oct. 1753- Jan. 1754

Fort Presque Isle

French Cr.

Fort Le Boeuf

Venango

Allegheny R.

Murthering
Town

PENNSYLVANIA

Ohio R.

Logstown

Shannopin's Town

"The
Forks"

Frazier's Cabin

Turtle Creek

Susquehanna R.

Gist's
Settlement

Wills Cr.

Red Stone Creek
(now Uniontown)

Wills Creek (now Fort Cumberland)

Monongahela R.

MARYLAND

Potomac R.

ALLEGHENY MTS.

Shenandoah R.

Alexandria
Mount Vernon
Belvoir

VIRGINIA

BLUE RIDGE

Rappahannock R.

Fredericksburg
Ferry Farm

CHESAPEAKE BAY

James R.

Richmond
Williamsburg

0   100 miles

0   150 km.

The land, he wrote, was "extremely well situated for a fort as it has absolute command of both rivers."

With his practiced surveyor's eyes, he also noted that "the Land at the Point is 20 to 25 feet above the common surface of the water, and a considerable Bottom of flat, well timbered land all around it, very convenient for building."

He took notice of the rivers, too.

"The Rivers are each a Quarter of a Mile, or more, across," he wrote, "and run . . . at very near right angles."

The Allegheny, he said, was "very rapid and swift," while the Monongahela was "deep and still."

The next day, the other four men and their horses arrived on the far shore of the Allegheny. Despite the swiftness of the water, they were able to cross safely to where Washington awaited them on the "Point."

Now, with his group together again, he had but seventeen miles to go to reach Logstown, the site of a major Indian village.

It was here, according to John Frazier, that he might be able to convince the Indians to lead him safely to the French.

The meeting with the Indians, if it took place as planned, was to be George Washington's first major effort at diplomacy.

If it failed, so would his mission.

Logstown was the home of many Indian families, most of them members of the Shawnee, Delaware, and Mingo tribes.

Logstown (near Ambridge, Pennsylvania) was also the village where Washington was told he would meet Chief Tanachariston, called "Half-King" by the British and French.

Half-King, a wily Seneca, was a sachem, or peace chief, and a representative of the Six Nations, the powerful ruling body for many of the tribes in the upper Ohio area. And since he had once signed an agreement that seemed to give the Ohio Company the right to build on Indian land, he was considered Britain's most important ally.

Furthermore, it was Half-King who had gone to the French and tried to persuade them not to extend their line of forts into the Ohio Valley.

When Washington and his group arrived in Logstown, they spent their first hours setting up camp and caring for the horses. As they did so, a colorful Irish trader named John Davison suddenly rode in from his cabin on the far side of the village and introduced himself.

Davison, Washington discovered, was popular among the Indians because he was fluent in their many tongues—all spoken with an Irish brogue!

When Washington offered to hire him as an interpreter, Davison readily accepted, saying, "What a foin idea!"

Chief Tanachariston, a Seneca, was known to the English and French as "The Half-King." At a time when Indian allegiances were uncertain and inconsistent, Half-King turned out to be a valuable ally of Washington's.

Later, at Washington's request, Davison invited Half-King to visit their tent and "smoke a pipe."

Half-King accepted. And when all were finally seated cross-legged around Washington's campfire, Washington nudged Davison.

"I'd like to know as much as possible about his meeting with the French Commandant," Washington said.

"I'm na so sure he'll tell us," Davison warned. "But I'll do me best."

Half-King was silent for a long time after Davison posed his question in the Indian tongue.

Finally, he began to speak slowly and carefully, as though he wanted to make certain Washington understood every word. And this, according to Washington's diary, is what Half-King said he told the French Commandant just a month before the Virginian's arrival in Logstown:

"Fathers, I am come to tell you your own speeches, what your own mouths have declared.

"Fathers, you, in former days, set a silver basin before us, wherein there was a leg of beaver, and desired all the nations to come and eat of it, to eat in peace and plenty, and not be churlish to one another; and that if any such person should be found to be a disturber, I here lay down by the edge of the dish a rod, which you must scourge them with; and if your father should get foolish, in my old days, I desire you may use it upon me as well as others.

"Now, fathers, it is you who are the disturbers in this land, by coming and building your towns and taking it away unknown to us, and by force.

"Fathers, we kindled a fire a long time ago at a place called Montreal, where we desired you to stay, and not to come and intrude upon our land.

I now desire you may dispatch to that place; for it is known to you, fathers, that this is our land and not yours.

"Fathers, I desire you hear me in civilness; if not, we must handle that rod which was laid down for the use of the obstreperous. If you had come in a peaceable manner, like our brothers the English, we would not have been against your trading with us as they do; but to come, fathers, and build houses upon our land, and to take it by force, is what we cannot submit to."

Washington glowed with satisfaction as Half-King paused to puff on his pipe. But his stomach constricted and he became tense as Half-King went on:

"Fathers, both you and the English are white, we live in a country in between; therefore, the land belongs to neither one nor the other. But the Great Being above allowed it to be a place of residence for us; so, Fathers, I desire you to withdraw, as I have done our brothers the English.

"I lay this down as a trial for both, to see which will have the greatest regard to it and that side we will stand by, and make equal shares with us."

Now, Half-King's voice rose in anger. "Our brothers the English have heard this," he said, "and I come now to tell it to you; for I am not afraid to discharge you off this land!"

Half-King indicated that was the end of what he had to say to the French. But Washington pressed his guest with this question.

"And what, my brother, was the Commandant's reply?"

"He said he would not hear me!" Half-King fairly shouted. And then he described the French General's words in this way:

"I am not afraid of flies or mosquitos, for Indians are such as these; I tell you, down that river I will go, and build upon it according to my command. If the river is blocked up, I have a force sufficient to burst it open, and tread under my feet all that stand in opposition, together with their alliances."

The General, said Half-King angrily, then declared:

"The Ohio Valley is my land and I will have it!"

That night, Washington, Gist, Davison, and van Braam discussed Half-King's speech and pondered their next move.

"Obviously, he knows where to find the French," van Braam commented.

"Sure he does," Gist said. "But he'll never take us to them."

"Why not?" van Braam asked.

"You know what he said!" Gist exploded, annoyed.

"But he seemed to think we were the lesser of two evils," Washington commented thoughtfully.

"Maybe," Gist said, "but that don't mean he'll agree to giving us an escort."

Van Braam wasn't convinced. "Why not?" he asked again.

"Because he knows even if he wanted to, the other Chiefs won't back him up," Gist insisted. "And if he asked 'em and they said 'no,' he would hate himself. Why? Because he's a proud man."

"But suppose all the Chiefs agree?"

"Then you'd get your escort," Gist said. "But how are you gonna get 'em to agree?"

"I'll go and ask them directly," Washington said. And when Gist made a face, he added, "What have we got to lose? We either get an escort or push on without one."

"Without one, you'll never see Mount Vernon again," Gist warned.

"Let's give it a try," Washington said. Then, looking directly at Davison he said, "Tell Half-King I want to meet with the Council."

"I'll see what can be done," Davison said with a nod.

Davison quickly left Washington's tent in search of Half-King. Returning an hour later he would only say, "Well now, it's like this — they'll be willin' to listen to what ye has to say."

The next morning, with Davison at his side, Washington met with Half-King and several other Indian chiefs in the council house at Logstown.

Since he had asked for the meeting, he was the first to speak.

"Brothers," he said through Davison, "by order of your brother, the Governor of Virginia, I am sent with all possible dispatch to visit and deliver to the French Commandant a letter of very great importance to your brothers the English; and I dare say to you, their friends and allies.

"I was desired, brothers, by your brother the Governor to call upon you, the sachems of the nations, to inform you of it, and to ask your advice and assistance to proceed to the nearest and best road to the French."

He said he would also like the sachems to provide him with an escort "to be a safeguard against those French Indians who have taken up the hatchet against us."

"I have spoken thus," he went on, "particularly to you, brothers, because his Honor, our Governor, treats you as good friends and allies and holds you in great esteem."

To confirm and underscore his remarks, Washington solemnly presented the sachems with a string of wampum.

Belts of wampum, usually made of shells, were used by Indians as money, gifts, and ceremonial offerings. The wampum marked with four towns that Half-King was determined to spitefully throw back at the French may have resembled this one.

After the wampum was graciously accepted, Half-King rose from his place and, looking directly at Washington, said:

"Now, my brother, in regard to what my brother the Governor has desired of me, I return you this answer; I rely on you as a brother ought to do, as to you saying we are brothers and one people. We shall put heart in hand and speak to our fathers the French concerning the speech they made to me. And you may depend that we will endeavor to be your guard."

Washington smiled appreciatively, but the smile faded when Half-King told him he could not leave immediately.

"We must wait," Half-King said.

"Wait for what?" Washington asked impatiently.

Half-King said they must wait for an important belt of wampum — a peace belt given him by the French.

"There are four towns marked on it," Half-King explained. "We wait until it comes from another village. Then, when we meet the French, I shall throw it in their faces!"

Washington started to protest, but Davison caught him by the arm.

"If he keeps his word, ye see, it means all agreements with them French will be canceled," Davison said softly.

Reluctantly, Washington held his tongue.

Washington, impatient to get on with his journey, decided to call on Half-King the next evening and try to persuade him to call in a guard so they could be on their way.

When he and Davison got to the council house, however, he discovered there was a raucous meeting going on inside. There was nothing to do but wait.

As Washington paced nervously back and forth in front of the little log building, the heated wrangling within went on for the better part of an hour.

"What's going on?" Washington asked Davison.

"They be arguin' about who's going with us and who ain't," Davison said.

Suddenly, all was quiet.

Davison stepped close to Washington and whispered, "We'll be knowin' now pretty soon, lad," he said.

Sure enough, a brave beckoned for them to enter the meeting place. Trying to hide his concern, Washington seated himself in an open spot in the silent circle of Chiefs.

After a few moments, Half-King announced that he and two other Chiefs and one of their best hunters would be their convoy.

"But we need a stronger guard than that!" Washington protested.

"My brother, you must realize that a larger group would alarm the French and their friends," Half-King explained patiently. "They might think we are coming to make war. That would be very dangerous."

Washington nodded. "Perhaps you are right," he said.

Now he wanted to know how soon they could leave Logstown.

When the peace belt arrives, he was told.
Dejectedly, Washington returned to his tent.

Later that night Davison awakened Washington with some news.

"The belt has arroived," he said with a smile.

With a sigh of relief, Washington went back to sleep.

ᐁᐁ Early on the morning of November 30, 1753, Washington rode out of Logstown with Half-King at his side.

Behind were Davison, van Braam, and Gist, two other Chiefs, Jeskakake and White Thunder, the four white helpers, and the pack train. The lone Indian hunter acted as a rear guard.

Since the shortest and best trail to Le Boeuf had been made impassable by heavy snows, Washington's party took a longer, more circuitous route, a route that would first lead them to Venango, an old Indian village.

It took about five days to travel the seventy miles to Venango (now a part of Pennsylvania), which is situated at the mouth of French Creek and the Allegheny River.

Topping a hill above the village, Washington reined his horse in so sharply that the animal reared.

"Gist!" he roared over his shoulder.

When Gist trotted up, Washington pointed down the hill to a small log house. A French flag flew from the roof!

"What do you make of that?" Washington asked.

"That's Frazier's old house," Gist responded. "He was on the wrong side so the French drove him out. Looks to me like they decided to move into the place."

Turning to Half-King, Washington asked, "Were there any French in the village when you passed through a few weeks ago?"

Half-King shook his head. "No French," he said.

Having been warned repeatedly that the loyalty of Indians was never secure, Washington insisted that Half-King and the rest of his escort establish camp and remain hidden in the woods while he, Gist, Davison, and van Braam rode down the hill to investigate.

As the four dismounted and approached the house, Washington remarked, "Maybe this is as far as we need to go."

"I wouldn't count on it," van Braam said.

Washington knocked on the door with the butt of his pistol and called out, "Anybody in there?"

The door flew open. A French officer stood face-to-face with Washington. "*Mon dieux!*" the startled officer gasped.

Before he could say another word, van Braam stepped forward. In the torrent of French words and emphatic gestures and bows that followed, the officer invited all to enter.

Inside were two more officers. As introductions flew about, Washington caught the name "Joncaire," a name that set off an alarm in the back of his mind.

Suddenly he remembered: This was Philip Thomas Joncaire, Sieur de Chabert. Despite the title, Joncaire had been raised by the Senecas, as was his father before him. Because of this, it was said that Joncaire had more power among the Indians than any other white man in America!

"We better keep Half-King away from that fellow," Washington muttered to Davison with a nod toward Joncaire.

"Aye," Davison agreed.

Joncaire and his friends politely invited Washington, van Braam, Davison, and Gist to stay for dinner, an invitation the group promptly accepted.

As soon as all were seated, Washington said to Joncaire, "I suppose you are wondering why we are here."

"Well, it is not every day we have an Englishman come knocking at our door in this part of the world," Joncaire laughed. "And I know this is not a social call. So why did you come?"

"I have a letter for you from my Government," Washington replied. "I hoped to have you read it and give me an answer."

"Ah, but it is not me you want," Joncaire responded. "The man to see such a letter is the Commandant, my superior officer. And if you wish to see him, you must go north to Le Boeuf."

"Then you can't accept the letter?"

"Ah, but *non!*" Joncaire cried. "Come, let us eat and forget about these Governments!"

During dinner, the French consumed a great deal of wine. This not only enlivened their spirits but loosened their tongues.

"Our objective is to take possession of all of the Ohio," Joncaire said with a smile of confidence at one point. Turning directly to Washington and banging the table for emphasis, he added, "And by God, we will do it!"

The French, he boasted, already had established a line of forts that extended northward to Montreal, Canada, a distance of seven hundred miles.

"Find out where they are," Washington said to van Braam. After another exchange, van Braam said, "The first one below the border is at Presque Isle (now Erie, Pennsylvania). Next is Le Boeuf, a third at Niagara, and the last—so far—is here."

"That's four," Washington said thoughtfully. Suddenly, he understood. These were the four towns on the wampum belt that Half-King vowed to throw at the French!

When Washington whispered this realization to Gist, the grizzled woodsman agreed. "If we can keep him away from Joncaire, maybe he'll do it," he whispered.

Just then, Half-King and the other Chiefs entered the house without knocking.

They had come to join the party.

Joncaire greeted the Indians with great ceremony and, laughing and gesturing, talked to them at length in their own language.

At the same time, Joncaire pressed food, wine, liquor, and small gifts on his new guests.

Despite his alarm, Washington could do no more than warn Half-King through Davison that he should not be taken in by "cheap gifts and liquor."

"He says na' to worry," Davison reported. "He has the wampum with him and he still says he will throw it in their faces."

But, as Washington noted in his diary, Joncaire "made several trifling Presents and applied Liquor so fast they were soon rendered incapable of the Business they came about . . . ."

Fearing the worst, Washington left what had become a wild party long before it ended. The wampum, of course, never left Half-King's belt.

The next morning, however, things changed dramatically.

"The Half-King came to my Tent, quite sober," Washington wrote in his diary. "He insisted that I should stay and hear what he had to say to the French."

But Washington said no; they should leave immediately for Fort Le Boeuf. There, Half-King could give his speech to the new Commandant, a much higher officer than Joncaire.

But Half-King was adamant. And so, after a Council fire was lighted, he sat across from Joncaire and spoke at length about how the Indians felt betrayed by the French. Then he took the wampum belt from his pouch and thrust it at Joncaire.

With profuse apologies, Joncaire said he could not accept the belt because he didn't have the authority to do so.

Very well, Half-King responded haughtily, he would go with the British to Fort Le Boeuf and throw the belt at the Commandant. That, he said, would end their relationship forever.

With a sigh of relief, Washington left the Council fire. Within the hour, he and his party were on their way to Fort Le Boeuf.

And riding beside him—still an ally—was Half-King.

For the Virginians and Indians trying to reach Fort Le Boeuf that winter of 1753, traveling conditions could not have been worse.

Hour after hour, from daylight to dark, they were buffeted by heavy rains and snows. And often, for every mile gained, two would be lost as they detoured swamps, swollen creeks, and flooded areas.

The sixty-mile journey, which in modern times would take less than two hours, took four and one-half days.

But at last—on the evening of December 11—they reached the fort and made camp for the night on the banks of a stream just across from its outer walls.

Early on December 12, Washington put on the wrinkled uniform he had carried in his baggage all the way from Williamsburg, buckled on his sword, and met with the Commandant, Legardeur de St. Pierre, a knight of the Military Order of St. Louis.

"He is an elderly Gentleman, and has much the Air of a Soldier," Washington noted in his diary, adding: "He was sent over to take command immediately upon the death of the late General [Marin] and arrived here seven days before me."

On meeting the Commander, Washington "acquainted him with my business" and presented Dinwiddie's letter.

At that moment, through these two interme-
diaries meeting in the wilderness, King George II
of England spoke to King Louis XV of France.

On receiving Dinwiddie's letter, St. Pierre and
his officers held a council of war to study it and
prepare a reply.

During the next twenty-four hours, as the
Council met, Washington, mindful of his order to
assess the strength of the French Army, wan-
dered around the fort making mental notes of everything he saw.

The fort, he wrote later, was situated on a
fork of French Creek where "four houses com-
pose the sides; the Bastions are made of Piles
driven into the ground and about 12 feet up, and
sharp at the top, with Port-Holes cut for cannon
and Loop-Holes for small arms . . . ."

He also noted that within the fort, there was
a guardhouse, chapel, and "Doctor's Lodgings."

The soldiers' barracks—made of logs—were
located outside the fort, as were "stables" and a
"Smith's Shop."

He estimated there were, ". . . according to
the best judgement I could form, . . ." a hundred
men at the fort, exclusive of the officers.

Washington and his men also made a count of
the number of canoes that were on hand: ". . .
there were 50 of Birch Bark, 170 of Pine; besides
many others were blocked out, in Readiness to
make . . . ."

This was clear evidence that the French planned to launch a major invasion into the Ohio Valley in the spring.

Not long after he gathered all this information, he was summoned to the Commandant's quarters and handed a letter to be given to Governor Dinwiddie.

He knew what the letter said without even reading it.

The French reply to Dinwiddie's demand that they leave Virginia's western frontier had become almost irrelevant.

What mattered now was the knowledge that the French planned an aggressive campaign to the south in the spring, a campaign that, should it succeed, would give them complete control of the Ohio Valley.

Williamsburg and London, Washington realized, must be warned. And quickly!

If the warning came too late, Britain and its colonists would have little chance of stopping the French, or of mounting a counteroffensive.

But the weather refused to cooperate with Washington and his small party. While St. Pierre's Council of War was in progress, the temperature dropped and a heavy snowfall blanketed the area.

"It doesn't matter," Washington insisted. "We can't wait. We've got to get back with the news!"

Since the horses were getting weaker every day for lack of food, Washington decided to send them, unloaded, ahead to Venango with van Braam and his four helpers.

"Gist, Davison, and I will follow in canoes," he told van Braam.

After getting van Braam on his way, Washington turned his attention to Half-King.

"When," he wanted to know, "will you give the wampum belt with the four towns on it to the Commandant?"

"Soon," Half-King said. "But we will meet in private."

The meeting took place the next day. When it was over, Half-King announced that the French Commandant had refused to take the belt.

"He made many promises of love and friendship," Half-King said. "He says he wants to live with us in peace and trade with us. As proof of his intentions, he is sending much goods to Logstown for us."

Washington was furious, but hid his anger.

"I saw that every stratagem which the most fruitful brain could invent was practiced to win the Half-King to [the French's] interests," he wrote in his diary.

The "stratagem" included promises of guns and liquor.

Finally, after a two-day delay, Washington persuaded the Indians to leave Fort Le Boeuf with him.

However, going down the river in canoes proved to be extremely trying and dangerous. Several times, one canoe or another was almost staved in by rocks.

And, quite often, those aboard the canoes had to step into the ice-cold river water and carry them over shoals.

At one point, an ice jam halted all further travel afloat, and the canoes had to be carried almost a mile overland before they could again be put down in open water.

The trip down the winding river traversed more than 130 miles — almost double the distance of the overland route — and took six days.

When Washington, Gist, Davison, and the Indians reached Venango, they found van Braam and the horses waiting for them.

Soon, however, Joncaire was up to his old tricks, lavishing praise, gifts, and liquor on Half-King and the other Indians.

On December 23, only one day after completing the harrowing river trip from Le Boeuf to Venango, Washington was ready to leave — with or without the Indians.

Before departing, however, he sought out Half-King.

"We must be on our way," he told Half-King. "Will you go with us?"

"No," the Chief replied with a straight face. "White Thunder is hurt and sick. I will stay with him for a few days and then take him to Logstown by canoe."

Washington shrugged his broad shoulders and pretended to understand, but he couldn't resist a warning: He hoped Half-King would not be fooled by Joncaire's flattery and gifts.

"Do not be concerned, my brother," Half-King said solemnly. "I know the French too well. When I get to the Forks I will make a speech for you to carry to His Honor the Governor."

Having made this translation, Davison told Washington he would return to Logstown with Half-King.

After expressing his appreciation to Davison and Half-King for their help, Washington and the rest of his entourage took the trail out of Venango. Soon, however, the horses became so weak that the riders had to dismount and lead them.

But progress was slow, too slow for Washington. On the third day out of Venango, he made a decision:

He and Gist would leave the trail the horses were obliged to follow and head directly through the forest for the Allegheny river — on foot.

"Accordingly," he wrote in the diary, "I left Mr. van Braam in Charge of our baggage, with money and directions to provide necessaries from place to Place for themselves and the horses."

Now, taking his "necessary papers" he "Pulled off my Cloaths" and put on an Indian walking dress.

Reluctantly, Gist did the same. And on December 26, Washington and Gist, with packs on their backs and each carrying a musket, struck out through the woods.

At that point, they were still hundreds of miles from civilization with nothing to guide them but the sun, the stars, and a compass.

On the first day after leaving van Braam, Washington and Gist traveled some eighteen miles. That was more than twice the distance they had been able to cover with the caravan the day before.

But the harsh pace through heavy snow and frigid weather caused both men to suffer greatly—Washington with sore feet, Gist from frostbite. To make matters worse, all the creeks and runs they came across were frozen. This meant that the only water they could get to drink was from melted snow, but then only after a fire had been built.

Still, they went on, the early part of their route taking them in a southeasterly direction to an Indian village called Murthering Town. Here they met a young Indian who called Gist by his Indian name and seemed very friendly.

"He's asking too many questions," Gist grumbled after he and the Indian talked.

"What kind of questions?" Washington wanted to know.

"He's asking about our horses. Wants to know where we left them. And why. He also wants to know where we're going."

Naively, Washington thought such questions were perfectly natural. To Gist's amazement, he asked whether the Indian could take them on a direct route to Shannopin's Town, an Indian village near the Forks.

Reluctantly, Gist spoke to the Indian again.

"He said he'd be happy to," Gist reported. "But I wouldn't advise it."

"Why not?"

"I think he's one of Joncaire's Indians," Gist said darkly.

But Washington brushed aside Gist's reservations and insisted on hiring the Indian as a guide.

"We'll save time by following someone who knows the way," he argued.

"Yes," Gist said. "But he could lead us into a trap or kill one or both of us in our sleep."

But there was only one thing on Washington's mind: getting to Williamsburg as fast as possible.

Gist finally gave in. And after a night's rest, the three started off, each carrying a musket and a small backpack.

At first, with the Indian leading the way, they moved southeast, which Washington and Gist judged to be the right direction.

Before long, however, the Indian began edging the party northeast. This made Washington and Gist suspicious.

"Tell him we want to camp at the next water," Washington said.

When Gist conveyed this to the Indian, he became annoyed and spoke rapidly to Gist.

"He says there are Ottawa Indians in these woods and they'll scalp us if we lay out. He wants to take us to his cabin which he says is only a little way off."

The trio moved on.

Late in the day, as they moved through a clearing in the woods, the Indian suddenly stopped and again spoke to Gist.

"What now?" Washington asked.

Gist laughed rather sardonically. "He wants to carry your gun! Says it will make it easier for you to walk."

"No!" Washington said with an emphatic shake of the head.

The Indian understood. With a crestfallen look and a shrug of the shoulders, he turned away. But then—without a word and at a distance of less than twenty feet—he suddenly whirled on the two white men, raised his own gun, and fired!

With the echo of that single shot still ringing in their ears, Washington and Gist hurled themselves upon the Indian and brought him crashing to the snow-covered and frozen earth.

Miraculously, neither man had been touched by the ball that blazed from the Indian's musket.

As the would-be murderer struggled beneath the weight of the two men, Gist whipped out a hunting knife with one hand and took a fistful of the Indian's hair with the other.

"No!" Washington said as Gist was about to cut the Indian's throat.

Gist was furious. "If we don't kill him, what do we do with him?"

"Let him go," Washington said quietly.

"We can't! He'll follow us and pick us off one-by-one!"

"We'll take his gun."

"That won't stop him. He's got friends out there. And he'll have them on our trail in no time."

"We've got to get rid of him somehow."

"I know," said Gist. Now he asked the Indian if the shot was an accident.

The Indian nodded vigorously.

Feigning satisfaction, Gist let the Indian up. "Go to your cabin and get it ready for us."

The Indian, astonished at this sudden chance for freedom, bolted into the forest. As soon as he disappeared, Washington and Gist rushed away from the area.

Washington wrote in his diary that the two walked all night "without making any Stop" so the Indian's allies would be "out of reach the next day, as we were assured they would follow our Tract as soon as it was light . . . ."

Washington expected to find the Allegheny frozen, which meant they could escape pursuit and be safely in Shannopin's Town by dark.

But when they reached the river bank at mid-morning, they found the swift-moving Allegheny filled with hundreds of tumbling, roaring ice floes, some weighing as much as a ton!

"We'll never make it across," Gist said as he studied the turbulent river.

"We'd better or we'll lose our scalps," Washington said, looking back the way they had come.

"Sure. But how?"

"Build a raft."

"Let's get at it!" Gist said, realizing a raft offered the only possibility of escape.

Working feverishly with what Washington called "one poor hatchet," the two men trimmed and hauled trunks of fallen trees to the riverbank where they were fastened together with vines and saplings.

The difficult and arduous task took all day. In fact, the sun was just going down when they launched the raft and climbed aboard.

Holding long poles and standing at either end of the slippery raft, Washington and Gist pushed hard for the opposite shore.

Suddenly, as the two men twisted and bobbed their way forward, Washington spied an especially large ice floe bearing speedily down on the raft.

"Hold her back!" he called to Gist as he dug his own pole in. But it was too late. Instead of flowing safely by, the floe hit his pole and threw him into the water.

Luckily, he was close enough to the raft to catch hold of one of the logs in his big hands. After a short struggle, he climbed wearily back aboard.

With only one setting pole between them, however, they were unable to move the raft in any direction but downstream. The situation seemed hopeless.

"Look!" Washington suddenly shouted as they were swept along.

He pointed ahead and to the left. What he saw was an island, one that would soon lie between them and the far shore.

Recounting his and Gist's ordeal of navigating the Allegheny River, Washington noted in his diary, ". . . we were jammed in the ice in such a manner that we expected every moment our Raft to sink, and ourselves to perish."

"If we're lucky, we might get close enough to swim for it," Washington said.

"Now that's a warm thought," Gist grumbled as he tried to pole the raft closer to the island.

Coming abreast of the island, Washington and Gist leaped into the icy waters of the Allegheny and quickly swam ashore.

That night (about the 27th of December), it became so bitterly cold that all of Gist's fingers and some of his toes were seriously frostbitten.

But the drop in temperature proved a blessing in one respect; by daylight, the river was a solid sheet of ice.

As they quickly crossed the river, snow began to fall. Nevertheless, they hurried on to Frazier's, reaching the big, smelly cabin on December 30.

Despite the weather, which was worsening, the urgency of Washington's mission put them on the trail back to Gist's the next morning, New Year's Eve day.

Arriving there two days later, on January 2, 1754, Washington bought two horses, a saddle, and supplies. And even though he was unable to find a tent, he gave Gist a farewell hug and set out almost immediately for Wills Creek, reaching it after enduring "as fatiguing a journey as it is possible to conceive rendered so by excessive bad weather . . . ."

For the next several days, it either rained or snowed every day. Still, he moved steadily southeastward. Finally, on January 11, the exhausted young Virginian rode his weary horse up a long, winding lane that led not to Mount Vernon but to Belvoir, where he knew he would once again be in the company of vivacious Sally Fairfax.

On January 16, four days after leaving Belvoir and the warmth of the Fairfax family, he was in Williamsburg attending a meeting of the King's Council during which he "waited upon His Honour the Governor with the letter I had brought from the French Commandant, and [gave] an Account of the Proceedings of my journey . . . ."

"Well, Gentlemen," Dinwiddie said grimly after he had read the letter and heard Washington's report on his epic odyssey of seventy-eight days, "their intentions are now revealed. They mean to take military possession of the Ohio!"

Clearly, all realized that Washington's perilous round-trip to the western frontier had set the stage for a new and ugly drama: war.

Governor Dinwiddie knew that he must act quickly if he hoped to thwart French plans to move into the Ohio Valley.

On hearing Washington's report, he ordered the young officer to put his notes into narrative form so they could be published.

"I want this done within the next twenty-four hours," Dinwiddie said.

"But, sir . . . ." Washington began to protest.

"No 'buts,'" Dinwiddie interrupted. "We've

no time to lose. We've got to get a military force out there ahead of the French. If we don't, all is lost!"

While Washington hurriedly transcribed his notes, Dinwiddie called the King's Council to emergency session. Looking at the calender, he saw that the next scheduled meeting of the House of Burgesses was April 18. He promptly moved it forward to February 14.

He also took these steps:

★ Assumed authority to recruit two hundred soldiers immediately to protect a crew of one hundred workmen he had recently sent to the Forks to build a fort
★ Wrote strongly worded letters to Governors of other colonies urging them to immediately join the budding campaign against the French

Dinwiddie also made plans to ask the Assembly for authorization to recruit an additional four hundred troops when it convened. He was convinced that if the Governors and the Virginia Assembly responded as he hoped, he would have a force strong enough to keep the Ohio Valley in British hands.

To Dinwiddie's dismay, however, his warnings and pleas, even though supported by Washington's seven-thousand-word document, were greeted with a collective and suspicious yawn.

Many believed that Washington's tale was "fiction," concocted to protect the interests of the Ohio Company, in which Dinwiddie, Colonel

Fairfax, the late Lawrence Washington, and other prominent Virginians were involved. Others saw nothing to be concerned about, even if Washington's report was true.

Pushing doggedly ahead, Dinwiddie fired off orders to Washington and other militia commanders to begin recruiting the necessary manpower from each of Virginia's military districts.

Now he was faced with a critical question: Who would command this force? Colonel Fairfax, the only man with any significant military experience in Virginia, declined the post because of his poor health.

Would Washington take it?

Washington was flattered, but made a sensible decision. "I'm too young and inexperienced for such an important position," he said. But, he added, he would certainly be willing to serve as lieutenant colonel under "a skilled commander or man of sense."

While there may have been many "men of sense" in Virginia, there certainly were no "skilled commanders" nor soldiers of any kind with much military experience.

Nevertheless, on March 20, 1754, Washington received and accepted his commission. Overall command, he learned, went to Joshua Fry, hardly the "skilled commander" that Washington had hoped for.

Colonel Fry was a former college mathematics teacher and an engineer.

↻ **Y**oung Washington had no formal military training. Using common sense and what little military knowledge he had, however, he began in early March to organize and drill a force of 159 men in Alexandria, not far from Mount Vernon.

His little "army" consisted of homeless, penniless, unemployed draftees and the reluctant sons of farmers. When they reported for duty, many recruits were without shoes, stockings, or even shirts.

Washington's first task—and a difficult one—was to obtain uniforms, wagons, horses, and supplies for the dangerous mission they all faced. Undaunted, he plunged ahead, soon bringing some semblance of order to his ragged troops.

And it was lucky that he did. For in less than a month, he received this message from Governor Dinwiddie:

"March with what soldiers you have enlisted immediately to the Ohio. Colonel Fry will follow with additional troops."

The French, he was told, had already begun their drive south from Fort Le Boeuf.

"You are to act on the defensive," Dinwiddie's orders went on, "but in case any attempts are made to obstruct the works or interrupt our settlements by any persons whatsoever, you are to restrain all such offenders and in case of resistance to make prisoners of, or kill and destroy them.

"For the rest, you are to conduct yourself as the circumstances of the service shall require and to act as you shall find best for the furtherance of His Majesty's service and the good of his dominion."

At precisely 8 o'clock the next morning, April 18, 1754, Washington was on his way to Wills Creek, Virginia's western frontier.

And not many miles beyond that, to his first military encounter.

Washington began his march to the Ohio as soon as he had enough wagons (two) and supplies to make it to Winchester, almost one hundred miles northwest of Alexandria.

By then, he had divided his force into three companies, putting one of them under the command of his old friend Jacob van Braam.

Remarkably, these green troops averaged eleven miles a day for the first leg of their journey. At Winchester, however, the march came to a sudden halt. And for a reason that would bedevil Washington for the rest of his military career: lack of provisions and transport.

To travel through two hundred miles of wilderness to Wills Creek, Washington desperately needed more wagons and supplies. But the farmers and others who lived in and around Winchester were not very cooperative.

As a military commander acting in an emergency, Washington was empowered to take a drastic step: "impress" (seize and pay for) wagons and food. Reluctantly, he decided to do so.

"We have no choice," he told his officers. "We're losing too much time here."

Given their orders, his troops rushed about the area seeking supplies. But the wily farmers hid their best wagons and horses and gave grudgingly of their food.

"Out of seventy-four wagons impressed in Winchester," Washington wrote Dinwiddie, "we got but ten . . . ; some of them provided so badly with teams that the soldiers were obliged to assist them up the hills, although it was known they had better teams at home."

After a week's delay, he led his men and a train of twelve wagons out of Winchester in a northwesterly direction and began to do what no one had done before—cut a crude, one-lane road up and over the mountains and through heavily wooded areas.

Bone-weary and spent, Washington and his men arrived at Wills Creek some two weeks after leaving Winchester.

Just as they moved into the little town, a rider on a lathered horse rode directly to Washington and handed him a letter that contained this brief message from the commander of Dinwiddie's work force at the Forks:

"Overwhelmed by one thousand French troops . . . ."

The race for the Ohio, barely begun by the Virginians, was over.

ne 'bright spot gleamed from the blackness of the news brought by the courier.

Half-King, Washington learned, was the first to lay a log for the structure started by the Virginians at the strategic junction of the Monongahela and Allegheny.

And Half-King also sent important personal messages to the Governors of Virginia and Pennsylvania and to Washington.

"Have good courage and come as soon as you can," Half-King wrote to the Governors. "You will find us as ready to fight the French as you are yourselves. If you do not come to our assistance now, we are entirely undone and I think we shall never meet again. I speak with a heart full of grief."

In his note to Washington, Half-King said that if Washington thought it necessary, the two of them could go to the Governors with his plea for help.

The import of these words was clear:

Half-King, speaking for the Six Nations, was committing the Indians to join the British in ousting the French. To ignore his call for assistance would mean the loss of his allegiance and, Washington was convinced, any hope of repelling the invaders.

But how could Washington's tiny, inexperienced force hope to combat a thousand highly trained French regulars? Obviously, that would be impossible.

And so, during a council of war, it was decided that Washington and his troops should push as close as possible to the Forks and await reinforcements.

After sending Half-King's messages plus his own plans to Dinwiddie, Washington wrote the Indian chief that "your friend and brother is coming; be strong and patient. A small part of our army [is] making towards you, clearing roads for a great number of our warriors, who are ready to follow us, with our great guns, our ammunition and provisions. You should come as soon as possible to meet us on the road, and to assist us in Council."

He signed the letter twice. Once as "Lieutenant Colonel George Washington." Then as "Counotaucarious," a name given to him by Half-King. It meant "Towntaker."

$\mathcal{C\!\!\!\!\!\curvearrowright}$ Washington's next objective was an Ohio Company storehouse on Red Stone Creek, which was some forty miles south of the Forks.

"I am destined to the Monongahela with all the diligent despatch in my power," he wrote Dinwiddie. "We will endeavour to make the road sufficiently good for the heaviest artillery to pass, and when we arrive at Red-stone Creek, fortify ourselves as strongly as the short time will allow. . . ."

The storehouse, however, was almost a hundred miles away. And reaching it that April was incredibly difficult. For days, rain poured down on the weary convoy without letup.

The rain, of course, made for slippery, muddy footing and caused rivers and streams to flood. As a result, crossings were hazardous and often impossible.

Then, too, trying to move loaded wagons up and down mountains where no wheeled vehicles had ever gone before proved to be a horrendous task.

The "road" that Washington's men carved out of the wilderness was nothing more than a narrow, rough, rain-slicked, and muddy trail strewn with boulders, stumps, and holes that often were axle deep.

In another letter to Dinwiddie, Washington said: ". . . the great difficulty and labour that it requires to amend and alter the roads prevents our marching above 2, 3, or 4 miles a day and I fear we shall be detained some considerable time before it can be made good for the Carriages of the Artillery with Colo. Fry."

He noted in the same letter that he was almost in daily contact with trappers and traders fleeing the French and moving east to the safety of the more inhabited areas of Virginia. These individuals, he said, "concur that the French have been reinforced with 800" and that 600 were busy building a fort at the Forks, which they called "Duquesne" in honor of the Governor of Canada.

And even though the agonizing, tedious work of road-building exhausted both men and horses long before sundown each day, the determined twenty-two-year-old Lieutenant Colonel promised Governor Dinwiddie that "no diligence shall be neglected."

April passed and May came. Still it rained. On May 24, Washington's little army made camp at a place called Great Meadows (now Uniontown, Pennsylvania). They had now covered about half the distance to the storehouse on Red Stone Creek, his main objective.

Suddenly and unexpectedly, two Indians rode up to Washington's tent.

Silently, one of them dismounted and handed him a letter.

It was from Half-King.

⟡T⟡he letter was written for Half-King by the Irish trader John Davison. Davison's grammar and spelling were atrocious, but Half-King's intent was clear.

"To the forist, his Majestie's Commander of-fwerses—to hom this may concern," the letter read. "On acc't of a french armey to meat Mister Georg Wassionton therfor my Brotheres I deisir you to beawar of them for deisin'd to strik ye for-ist English they see ten deays since they marchd I cannot tell what nomber the half king and the rest of the chiefs will be with you in five dayes to consel, no more at present . . . ."

Washington promptly called his officers to his tent and held up the letter.

"It took me a while to figure this out," he said grimly. "But it's a warning from Half-King that a party of French are coming after us."

"How many?" van Braam wanted to know.

"He doesn't say," Washington answered. "But there is one good piece of news. Half-King and his chiefs are coming in for a council."

Anticipating an attack, Washington and his men searched the Meadows for a good place to make a stand. They found what Washington later described as "two natural gulleys" close together.

Here the men dug trenches as part of a crude, defensive position, then cleared the ground around it of brush and trees that might interfere with their marksmanship. Later, they would construct a palisades between the gulleys.

Washington called this place "Fort Necessity."

The next morning, May 27, Washington had another surprise. Christopher Gist, his companion of the previous winter, rode in. Gist had come from his trading post, which was located in a small Indian settlement about halfway between Great Meadows and the storehouse.

"I got here as soon as I could," he told Washington. "Yesterday noon, a French officer and fifty soldiers came into my settlement. I wasn't there. But the Indians told me they came down the Monongahela from Duquesne by canoe. They were in an ugly mood. Wanted to kill the cows and break up the place. The Indians talked them out of it and they left."

"Any idea where they went?" Washington asked.

"No. But I came across a lot of tracks on my way here."

"Do you think it's the same band?"

"No doubt about it."

"How far away were these tracks?"

"Five miles," came the ominous reply.

Fifty French soldiers only five miles away?

Washington promptly sent for Captain Peter Hog (pronounced Hohg).

After explaining what Gist had discovered, he said, "Take seventy-five men and see if you can find them. If you do, get back here as quickly as you can."

Hog was gone several hours, but could find no sign of the French.

Washington now hurriedly wrote a dispatch for Dinwiddie and handed it to Gist.

"Dinwiddie is on his way to Winchester," he said. "Please take this message to him and urge him to send reinforcements and supplies as soon as possible."

After their evening meal, the troops settled down for the night. At nine o'clock, however, an Indian brave slipped into the camp and went to Washington's tent.

It was Silverheels, one of Half-King's men.

Van Braam was summoned to speak to the Indian. After a brief conversation, van Braam told Washington, "He says Half-King is about six miles away. He says the Chief came on the tracks of two men. These tracks came from our camp and led to a hollow where he thinks the whole force is camped. He wants you to go to him immediately. Silverheels, he says, will lead you."

After putting the camp on full alert, Washington and forty of his men fell in behind Silverheels in single file. As they moved off in a northerly direction, it started raining. It rained harder and harder.

In the wet, extreme darkness, the troops often stumbled, fell, and became lost. Sometimes the party was delayed up to twenty minutes before it could move on.

As a result, Washington and his men didn't arrive at Half-King's camp until sunrise. By then, the rain had stopped.

With Half-King were Chief Monakatoocha, four Indians with rifles, and six armed with only bows, arrows, hatchets, and knives.

Half-King promptly called a brief council. With a stick, he made a series of marks on the ground.

"They are here," Half-King said. "And we are here."

The French camp, he said, was in a hollow. With the exception of one area, the ridges above were covered with rocks and woods.

It was decided that the soldiers and Indians would form a circle above the French camp. Washington, in the open area (where he could be seen from below), would give the signal to open fire from all sides.

By 8 A.M. on May 30, 1754, all were deployed as planned.

H

is musket loaded and ready, Washington moved cautiously out on the open ridge above the French camp. As he looked down, a startled Frenchman looked up and yelled, *"Ennemi!"*

The cry of alarm sent the French scrambling for their guns. Washington promptly called out as loudly as he could, "Fire!"

Simultaneously, he and his little force loosed a deafening volley on those below. Somehow, however, several shots were returned, most of them toward Washington and his exposed squad. (In a letter to his brother, Washington later said that he had heard the "whistle" of the bullets for the first time in his life and found it "charming.")

The fight lasted only twenty minutes. Ten of the French were dead, one was wounded, and several escaped. The rest threw down their arms. Washington's group suffered one dead and one wounded.

As the smoke of the battle drifted away, Washington had to restrain Half-King and his followers, all of whom were bent on collecting scalps. Half-King was outraged. He said the French had "boiled and eaten" his father. He wanted revenge!

Among the bodies was that of the French commander, Joseph Coulon, Sieur de Jumonville.

His death would haunt Washington for years.

After being marched back to Fort Necessity, two French officers insisted on knowing what Washington planned to do with them.

Speaking through van Braam, Washington said, "You are prisoners of war and you will be treated accordingly."

"War?" a Captain Druillon, second in command, shouted. "What war? We came in peace. We are ambassadors. We have come only to tell you to leave our territory. We demand that you send us safely back to Duquesne with escort!"

Papers found on Jumonville's body indicated that Druillon might be telling the truth. Dated May 23, 1754, and signed by a high-ranking officer named Pierre Pécaudy, Sieur de Contrecoeur, they were addressed to the commander of British troops.

"We only want peace," the paper said in effect. "You must leave our territory. If you do not do so, we will have no choice but to force you off our land."

On conferring with van Braam and Half-King, Washington rejected these statements, raising the following points:

★ The papers were a "cover" in case any of the French officers were captured.
★ The tracks of two Frenchmen led from Washington's encampment to where Jumonville and

the rest of his men were found. This showed that two men were spying on Washington's camp and reporting back to Jumonville.

★ If the French were on a peaceful mission, why did they hide themselves for so long?
★ And since when did "ambassadors" travel with such a large body of troops?
★ The French were on British soil.
★ The capture of a British possession at the Forks was certainly not a peaceful act. It was an act of war!

"No," Washington concluded. "You came within two miles of our camp. You came to find out where we were and in what strength. You then planned to communicate with your commander at Fort Duquesne, acquire a larger force, and attack us."

In short, Washington said, the captured French were spies.

"And you will be treated as spies!" he said.

It was a decision that turned out to have far-reaching implications.

Having sent the prisoners east to Winchester, then on to Williamsburg, Washington again had his men continue cutting the road to Red Stone Creek.

He also wrote several reports as well as letters to friends and family.

In a dispatch to Colonel Fry, who was still stuck in Winchester for a lack of wagons and provisions, Washington warned: "If there does not come a sufficient reinforcement, we must either quit our ground and retreat to you, or fight on very unequal terms, which I will do before I will give up one inch of what we have gained . . . ."

But the threat posed by the French was not his only problem. In addition to the numerous Indians already in his camp, Queen Aliquippa arrived. She said that she was afraid of being attacked by the French because of the role the Indians had played in Jumonville's death.

Obviously, Washington had no choice but to receive her. Unfortunately, Aliquippa brought some twenty-five families with her, most of them consisting of children and women.

The Indians, of course, put a severe strain on the food supply. On the morning of June 6, Washington was busy writing letters when the supply sergeant came to his tent.

"Excuse me, sir," he said after a discreet cough. "But you wanted to be kept informed about the food."

Washington braced himself. "How bad is it?"

"We are out of salt and flour and down to only a few milk cows," was the sergeant's ominous reply.

Slamming a fist on his writing table, a frustrated Washington uttered one word: "Damn!"

Ten minutes later, all but two of his wagons were on the way to the nearest settlements in search of food.

⁓Later that day (June 6), Christopher Gist returned from Wills Creek with startling news.

"Colonel Fry is dead," Gist told Washington. "Killed in a fall from his horse about a week ago."

Gist then handed Washington two dispatches from Dinwiddie. In one, Washington was named to replace Fry. In another, Dinwiddie said several "independent" companies of soldiers were on the way, the nearest under the command of Captain James Mackay.

The independents, Washington knew, were regulars in the British Army.

"I'll be glad to see them," he told Gist. "But they may present a problem."

He was right. When Mackay arrived, he refused to take orders from the newly appointed Colonel, even though his rank was three grades below Washington's.

Washington argued that Colonels were Colonels and Captains were Captains.

"Not so," Mackay replied coolly. "An officer commissioned by the King out-ranks any Colonial officer. And Governors cannot appoint a man to command an officer of His Majesty's troops. He doesn't have that power or authority."

"I see," said a seething Washington. "And what about your men, Captain?"

"What about them?"

"Can we put them to work on the road beside my troops?"

"Of course not!" came Mackay's response. "My men are professional soldiers, not laborers." Then Mackay added slyly, "Of course, they may be willing to work on the road if you're willing to pay them for such extra service."

"Captain Mackay, you and your men are already paid twice the amount we receive," Washington snapped. "To pay your men even more would lead to a mutiny!"

Mackay shrugged and went off to find a separate camp for his unit.

Following his original plan, Washington had his two remaining wagons loaded and began a march to Gist's settlement, which was as close to the Forks as he dared to go.

True to form, Mackay said he would stay in Great Meadows.

At Gist's, Washington put most of his force to work on the road and directed the rest to begin building a stockade. He then called for a council of various Indian tribes in an attempt to gain their allegiance.

The council was well attended. It included Shingiss, Chief of the Delawares, several representatives from the Shawnee tribe, eight Mingoes (who later turned out to be spies), Half-King, and forty members of the Six Nations.

Slowed by the translation of long speeches, the council went on for three days. To Washington's dismay, it was a failure.

The Shawnees, Mingoes, and Delawares simply disappeared without explanation. And despite Washington's pleas, Half-King and his people insisted on returning to Great Meadows.

But the next morning, Washington was cheered by the news that Chief Monakatoocha had burned Logstown (the Indian village Washington had passed through on his way to Fort Le Boeuf the previous year) and was taking his people south to Red Stone.

A few days later, Washington received this frightening message from the Chief:

"I have been near Fort Duquesne and heard eight hundred French and four hundred of their Indians will soon be moving to attack you."

$\mathcal{W}$as Monakatoocha's warning reliable? Would a force of 1,200 soon be descending on Washington's puny army? If so, when?

With these questions rolling about in his mind, Washington took an instinctive step: He called his men off the road and sent for Mackay.

Surprisingly, Mackay arrived at Gist's the next day. The British now had a combined force of four hundred.

In a hastily called council of war, Washington reviewed all the facts available to his command. Boiled down, they were as follows:

★ The French could travel rapidly and easily down the Monongahela almost to Gist's, enabling them to launch an attack in a few days.

★ If Monakatoocha's report was correct, the British were badly outnumbered.

★ There was only enough food for six days. The French could lay siege to the stockade and cut off supplies from Great Meadows. If that happened, Washington's forces could be starved into surrendering.

★ If the British somehow held off the French, then retreated, they could not survive Indian attacks in the forests.

★ By retreating to Fort Necessity, Washington's supply route could be shortened, that of the French lengthened and made more difficult.

★ The Indians still with Washington threatened to leave unless he ordered a return to Great Meadows.

The final decision? Retreat!

Desperate to put distance between themselves and the superior French army and French Indians, Washington's troops hurriedly organized their departure from Gist's early on June 29.

The items to be moved included nine wheeled swivel guns, ammunition, essential baggage, food, and a small herd of cattle.

Here's how this was accomplished:

★ The two wagons were quickly loaded with provisions of all sorts.

★ Washington and his officers gave up their horses. Stripped of saddles, the horses were loaded with ammunition.

★ Drovers were assigned to the cattle.

★ Ropes were attached to the heavy, cumbersome swivel guns so they could be hand-hauled.

Strung out for a mile, the army of four hundred men followed a rough, rocky, steeply uphill trail that took them through heavy woods and over numerous streams.

The agonizing and bitter daylight retreat of thirteen miles took the better part of three days. And during this period, the only food available consisted of parched corn and small portions of freshly slaughtered beef.

To add to the ordeal, Mackay and his independents haughtily refused to help with the guns, and his officers would not give up their horses. This attitude brought curses, cries of rage, and dark mutterings.

"Why should we do the work and not them?" one Virginian yelled out on the first day of the march.

"And why should they get more pay than us?" a companion then shouted.

Clearly, the sweating, panting troops were on the verge of mutiny. But their tall Colonel moved calmly along the line of march, offering words of comfort and understanding. Their anger and frustration subdued, the soldiers kept on with their assigned tasks.

On July 1, weak and half-starved, the marchers reached Fort Necessity. To their bitter disappointment, the wagons that Washington sent foraging for food before he left for Gist's had not returned.

After a brief greeting on Washington's arrival, Half-King said through an interpreter, "You will continue the retreat tomorrow, yes?"

"No," Washington said politely. "The men are too tired and weak to go on."

"But there is no food here," Half-King protested. "And we are not strong enough in numbers!"

"I have been promised reinforcements and food."

Fort Necessity was rough, primitive, and ill-equipped to stand up to the powerful French troops that descended upon it the morning of July 3, 1754. The modern-day reconstruction pictured here gives us an idea of its vulnerability.

"Promises!" Half-King barked. "There have been such promises before. And they were not kept."

"I know," Washington said wearily. "But we're staying. If they come, we'll fight it out."

"In that thing?" Half-King said mockingly, pointing to the entrenchments and stockade.

"Yes," said Washington.

Without another word, Half-King angrily strode away.

Within the next few hours, Washington's only Indian ally was gone.

$\mathcal{CD}$A s Half-King perceived, Fort Necessity was in a weak defensive position. It was surrounded by woods and rocks and easily reached by musket fire from higher ground.

But there was no time to relocate, so Washington put his weary men to work enlarging the stockade and adding to the trenches.

Most of the fields around the fort were marshy. The open ground to the south, however, was dry. This, thought Washington, is the way they will come.

Without Indians to scout the woods, Washington had to resort to posting sentinels both day and night at every possible approach to the fort.

During daylight, the only sounds around the encampment were those made by the troops as they worked on the defenses. At night, all was quiet.

At daybreak on July 3, a single shot from one of the outposts shattered the morning silence.

The French had been sighted!

$\mathcal{CD}$R ubbing sleep from their eyes, the Virginians scrambled to their positions. As they did so, it began to rain. Harder. And harder!

At 11 o'clock that morning, with their Indians whooping and hooting, three columns of French moved stealthily across the meadow from the south, just as Washington had expected.

Having formed a firing position in front of the trenches, Washington's soldiers were ready. At a distance of about six hundred yards, the French loosed a volley on the British line, hitting no one.

The British did not return the fire as the distance was too great.

Now, the French reloaded and advanced again.

"Back!" Washington yelled.

His men promptly wheeled and jumped down into the trenches. As they did so, the swivel guns, mounted on the parapet, opened up. The French immediately dropped to the ground and sought cover behind trees and rocks.

Firing only when they saw a good target, the British took a heavy toll among the French and Indians. But rainwater rose steadily in the trenches, and Washington's troops had difficulty keeping their powder and weapons dry.

From the surrounding woods and other places of hiding, the French soon had the upper hand. They not only killed and wounded about a third of Washington's force but also shot his cattle and horses.

Worst of all, the rain turned to a deluge. By mid-afternoon, water filled the trenches and even wet the powder boxes in the stockade.

By the time the sun went down, the British

were practically afloat and virtually without weapons; all their ammunition was soaking wet and useless.

Suddenly, there was a lull in the firing and a French voice called out:

"Voulez-vous parler?"

V an Braam was called to Washington's side.

"What do they want?" Washington wanted to know.

"They want to talk," was van Braam's answer.

Washington was suspicious. "I think they want to get a closer look at us so they can finish us off," he said. Then to van Braam, "Tell them 'no,' we don't want to talk."

Van Braam conveyed this to the French. There was a long silence, then another query:

"Can you send a man who speaks French to hear a proposal? On our word of honor he will be able to return safely."

Before responding, Washington and his officers quickly assessed their situation. It came down to this:

At least a third of his force was either dead or wounded.

Only two bags of flour were left.

Virtually all their powder was wet.

Their animals had been killed.

Clearly, they could not fight any longer.

"Van Braam, go and see what they have to say," Washington said grudgingly.

Under a white flag, van Braam proceeded slowly to the French line. It was still raining so heavily that he soon disappeared from Washington's view.

After a long period, van Braam returned.

"They want us to surrender," he said glumly. "The terms are on this paper."

With a sinking heart, Washington asked van Braam to read the French proposal.

As rain dripped from his hat and chin, van Braam shielded a candle and slowly and haltingly tried to make the French words understandable to his Commander.

Washington apparently caught the meaning of all but one word.

It was an omission he would live to regret.

According to van Braam's reading of the damp and blurred handwritten offer made by the French, these were its principal points:

★ Washington and his men could leave and return to the other side of the Alleghenies.

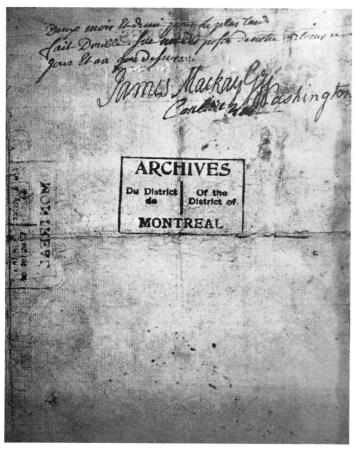

After Washington signed the surrender of Fort Necessity, he handed it to Captain Mackay. Always looking for a chance to assert his power, Mackay signed it boldly and at an angle in the open space above Washington's name.

★ They must promise not to build anything west of the Alleghenies for a year.
★ The defeated troops could take anything with them they wished, except arms and munitions.

★ The French would hold two hostages until the French prisoners Washington captured were returned to Fort Duquesne.
★ Washington could leave a doctor and eleven men behind to care for the wounded.

Easily understood, these terms, however, were preceded by an important paragraph that seems to have been glossed over. Under the heading "Capitulation," this paragraph (written in French) read: "Our intentions have never been to trouble the peace and good harmony which reigns between two friendly Princes, but only to avenge the assassination which has been done of one of our officers . . . ."

The officer referred to was Jumonville. And the man now calling for his revenge was the French Commander, Coulon de Villiers.

Villiers was Jumonville's brother.

For some reason, the word for assassination— *l'assassinat*—which appeared twice (once in a slightly different form) was translated as "loss" or "killing." Unaware of the true meaning of the word, and after quibbling over one or two points, Washington signed the document.

At daylight on July 4, just as the rain stopped, Washington and his weary, dejected troops began the depressing preparations that had to be made before they could leave Fort Necessity.

Since all the horses had been killed, both officers and men now faced the reality that they would have to walk back over the mountains to Wills Creek if they hoped to live.

This meant they could carry only food and sidearms. Virtually everything else had to be destroyed or left behind.

Final arrangements were also made to turn over the two hostages to the French. Chosen as escorts after much debate among Washington's officers were van Braam and Captain Robert Stobo.

As the pair were about to leave for the French camp, Washington offered van Braam a scarlet waistcoat and an elegant broadcloth coat trimmed with silver. Both had been carefully transported in Washington's baggage and were in excellent condition.

"I can't carry these home, so you might as well have them," Washington said with a smile.

Van Braam was delighted. But the articles were not a gift. Washington, always mindful of his funds, collected thirteen pounds from van Braam.

At about 10 o'clock, Washington called his men to order. When the 293 officers and soldiers were in line, he marched them out of Fort Necessity with flags flying and to the beating of drums. Towed in their midst was a single cannon, which was soon to be abandoned.

This staged departure was part of a ritual known then as "the honors of war."

For Washington the surrender was mortifying. But there was more humiliation to come.

○○○ **D**uring the summer of 1754, Washington's name seemed to be on every tongue.

The colonies were shocked to learn, for example, that the young Virginia Colonel had been branded a murderer and an incompetent by Sieur Coulon de Villiers.

In a Paris publication the French Commander said: ". . . We made them consent to sign that they had assassinated my brother in his camp; we had hostages for the security of the French who were in their power; we made them leave their cannon, nine pieces; we destroyed their horses and cattle and made them sign that the favors granted were evidence that we wanted to use them as friends . . . ."

From Britain, too, there was harsh criticism of the young Colonel. "He should have avoided an engagement until all our troops were assembled," one critic said. Another, the Earl of Albemarle, noted that "Washington and many such may have courage and resolution but they have no knowledge and experience in our [military] profession; consequently there can be no dependence on them."

The Earl went on to say that the French could not be driven "back to their settlements" unless British officers were sent to the colonies to "discipline the militia and lead them on as a nation . . . ."

Another Englishman wrote that the capitulations at Fort Necessity signed by Washington ". . . were the most infamous a British subject ever put his hand to."

Even the King was said to have made disparaging remarks about Washington.

Many in Virginia, however, saw things differently. They seemed to realize that if Washington had been given the men, arms, and food he had repeatedly been promised, the campaign would have turned out differently.

As the *Virginia Gazette* said, "Thus have a few brave men been exposed, to be butchered, by the negligence of those who, in obedience to their Sovereign's command ought to have been with them many months before; and it is evidently certain, that had the Companies from New York been as expeditious as Captain Mackay's from

South Carolina, our camp would have been secure from the insults of the French, and our brave men still alive to serve their King and country . . . ."

Washington was also absolved of any guilt in connection with his signing of the "capitulation." It was the "treachery" of van Braam that caused him to sign, many said.

Significantly, when the General Assembly convened on October 21, it thanked Washington and all the officers of the campaign — except van Braam — for their "gallant and brave behaviour in the defense of their country."

Having arrived in Williamsburg that very day, Washington sent the Speaker of the House of Burgesses the following response:

"Nothing could give me and the officers under my command, greater satisfaction, than to receive the thanks of the House of Burgesses, in so particular and public a manner, for our behavior in the late unsuccessful engagement with the French, and we unanimously hope, that our future proceedings in the service of our country, will entitle us to a continuance of your approbation. I assure you, sir, I shall always look upon it as my indispensable duty to endeavor to deserve it."

Before long, however, circumstances dealt another severe blow to Washington's pride.

While in Williamsburg, Washington learned that Dinwiddie was in session with Governor Arthur Dobbs of North Carolina and Governor Horatio Sharpe of Maryland.

Dobbs, after a perilous twelve-week journey from England to Virginia, brought money and plans for another campaign to the Ohio.

Dobbs also delivered a Lieutenant Colonel's commission for Governor Sharpe, coupled with orders that Sharpe was to be in command of all colonial forces ". . . raised to protect His Majesty's Dominions from the encroachments and devastations of his presumptuous enemies," meaning the French.

Subsequently, Washington learned that his Virginia regiment was to be broken up and changed to independent companies. The companies were then to be commanded by Captains.

Obviously, Washington would lose his rank as a Colonel. And if he accepted the demotion, he would still have to take orders from officers with a King's commission.

"In short," he was to say later in indignation, "every Captain bearing the King's commission, every half-pay officer, or other, appearing with such a commission, would rank before me."

As he saw it, there was only one course of action open to him.

He resigned.

⟨⟨⟩⟩ **A**s the new Commander in Chief, Governor Sharpe was unwilling to accept Washington's resignation. He realized that the young army officer's experience would be invaluable in the coming campaign.

In the stilted but polite language used in Colonial times, Sharpe asked Washington to reconsider. In effect he said, "You can keep the title of Colonel, and I will see to it that you will not have to take orders from those who would have had a lower rank during your command."

As Washington thought about Sharpe's proposal, much of what had happened in the past year must have crossed his mind:

- ★ the difficult round-trip as a courier between Williamsburg and Fort Le Boeuf during the previous winter, a journey during which he twice nearly lost his life;
- ★ the hardships and frustrations endured during his return to the frontier and beyond with green troops, scanty provisions, and lack of support;
- ★ the troubles with Mackay;
- ★ the political struggles with the Indians;
- ★ the failure of contractors to deliver food and supplies;
- ★ the failure of Dinwiddie and the other Governors to send reinforcements when he needed them;
- ★ the stigma of being accused of murdering Jumonville;

* the humiliation of surrender in the blood and mud of Fort Necessity;
* the dead, the wounded, and the near starvation of the survivors;
* and now, the arbitrary loss of rank.

Finally, he wrote to Sharpe: "You make mention in your letter of my continuing in the Service, and retaining my Colonel's Commission. This idea has filled me with surprise; for if you think me capable of holding a Commission that has neither rank or emolument annexed to it; you must entertain a very contemptible opinion of my weakness, and believe me to be more empty than the Commission itself . . . ."

He said that if he had the time, he could "enumerate many good reasons, that forbid all thoughts of my returning."

He added that he was consoled by the fact "that I have opened the way when the smallness of our numbers exposed us to the attacks of a Superior Enemy; That I have hitherto stood the heat and brunt of the Day, and escaped untouched in time of extreme danger; and that I have the thanks of my Country, for the Services I have rendered it."

In closing, Washington made it known that he was reluctant to leave the military. "My inclinations," he said, "are strongly bent to arms."

Still, his answer to Sharpe's offer was clear: thanks, but no thanks.

So ended the first phase of Washington's military career.

Although he had no way of knowing it, a second and more critical phase was about to begin.

"Major General Edward Braddock To Oust French!"

This electrifying headline jumped from the front page of the *Virginia Gazette* during the early winter months of 1754–1755.

And, as the *Gazette* jubilantly predicted, Braddock soon arrived in Williamsburg with two regiments of British regulars.

Greeted with much fanfare, and wined and dined by many of Virginia's leading families, Braddock immediately began making plans for the campaign that included filling out his regiments with Colonial carpenters, cooks, herdsmen, farriers (men who shoed horses), foot soldiers, and officers.

Braddock, a short, pudgy man of sixty, also bustled aggressively about demanding that the colonists supply his troops with horses, wagons, cattle, and a great quantity and variety of items needed to sustain an army in the field.

His presence and well-publicized activities raised a natural question in virtually every home and tavern in Virginia:

*Major General Edward Braddock, supreme commander
of British forces in America, sought out Washington's
help in the campaign against the French. However, he
would later ignore Washington's advice and pay for it
with his life.*

Would George Washington be joining General Braddock?

No one, it seemed, dared asked Braddock directly. As for Washington, he chose not to answer when queried. One evening at the Fairfaxes, however, where he was spending a great deal of time, he finally felt obliged to offer an explanation.

"I thought I'd wait to see if the Governor would act on my behalf," he said as the family, including Colonel Fairfax, George William, and Sally, gathered around him at the fireplace after dinner.

"He will," Colonel Fairfax said.

"I'm not so sure," Washington said. "We've had a bit of a disagreement, you know."

"Oh?" the Colonel said in surprise.

"He's angry because I resigned. And I'm just as angry because he has held up my back pay."

"Is that so?" Colonel Fairfax said. "Well, I'll have a word with him about that!"

"Please don't, sir," Washington said.

"Why not?" Sally Fairfax wanted to know.

Washington took a deep breath and faced the group. "There's another problem."

"And what's that?" George William asked.

"The answer is here in the *Gazette*," Washington said, then proceeded to read from an article on the front page: '. . . all troops serving by commissions signed by General Braddock shall take rank before all troops which may serve by commission from the Colonial Governors . . . .'

"So you see," said Washington, "nothing has changed. The British high command still see Colonial officers and men as inferior to their regulars."

In other words, Washington made clear, he would not take orders from a British regular of lower rank should he join Braddock as a Colonial officer.

"It's a matter of principle," he said.

And principles, as Washington was to demonstrate over and over, were important.

⌒⌒⌒ For the next several weeks, Washington tried to put all thoughts of the military buildup going on in Virginia and elsewhere out of his mind.

With Sally's help he concentrated instead on making Mount Vernon more comfortable and livable. Together, for example, they selected furniture, floor coverings, and drapes for the little house he had leased from Anne Fairfax Lee—the house that was now his home.

But when he learned that a young man from Massachusetts and another from Pennsylvania had joined. Braddock as personal aides at the request of their respective governors, his resolve to remain aloof from the activity in Williamsburg weakened.

Since Virginia was the biggest colony, why didn't Dinwiddie recommend another aide to Braddock? And why couldn't he be that aide? For Washington, such a position offered these advantages:

★ He would have no troops to command.
★ He would take orders from only one person — the General himself.
★ His main duty would be to deliver the General's orders to others, giving him a golden opportunity to learn how a modern army functioned.

It was a perfect solution to his dilemma!

By late February, he gave up all hope of having Dinwiddie speak up for him. So he wrote to Braddock himself, offering his services as a "volunteer." In doing so, however, he stuck to his position about the matter of military rank.

On March 14, he received this reply:

Sir: The General having been informed that you expressed some desire to make the campaign, but that you declined it upon the disagreeableness that you thought might arise from the regulation of command, has ordered me to acquaint you that he will be very glad of your company in his [military] family, by which all inconveniences of that kind will be obviated.

Sir, Your most obedient servant
Robert Orme, aide-de-camp

$\mathcal{I}$t was late March before arrangements could be made for Braddock and Washington to meet in Williamsburg.

Their meeting began smoothly and cordially. The General, of course, had been well briefed about his tall visitor and was anxious to have him on his staff.

"As I understand it, you would like to join us as an aide-de-camp," Braddock said as they sat alone in his office in the Governor's Palace.

"Yes," Washington said, "as a volunteer."

"That would be fine," Braddock said. "You'll report to me with the rank of Captain, the highest rank I'm authorized to confer on anyone."

"Thank you, your Excellency, that's certainly acceptable," Washington said. "But I have one or two reservations."

Braddock's eyebrows shot up in surprise. "Oh?"

"I have leased a farm near Alexandria. Since I will not be receiving any pay and am with limited funds, I must occasionally attend to my personal affairs."

"Can you be more specific?" Braddock said, getting a bit testy.

Washington then explained that whenever the Army became idle he would like a leave of absence to return to Mount Vernon if necessary. He also wanted to be free to resign at the close of the year's campaign.

"Conditions accepted," Braddock said briskly. "Report to me in Alexandria in one week."

It was a busy week for Washington. Among other things, he arranged for his brother Jack to take over Mount Vernon while he was gone.

But just as he was packed and ready to leave, there was a knock at the door. When he opened it, he was face-to-face with the last person in the world he expected to see: his mother.

Her lips tight, her eyes hard and blazing with anger, Mary Ball Washington immediately launched into a tirade as she moved through the front door of Mount Vernon.

"How can you, George?" she cried. "How can you go off and leave me again?"

"Now, Mother . . . ."

"Don't 'now, mother' me," she snapped. "You've done enough for your country. Let somebody else step forward now. This Braddock doesn't need you."

"But I want to go!" Washington protested.

"To get killed?"

"Of course not!"

"Then why?"

"Because the campaign will allow me to get to know how the Army functions from the very top."

"From 'the top!' " she mocked. "My, my."

"I'll be an aide to the General."

"An aide? Ha! You know what you'll be? A bootlicker! A bootlicker, that's what!"

The argument continued for several minutes. And while he patiently and politely listened to the objections that poured from his mother's lips, often between tears, Washington refused to change his plans.

Braddock's attempt to launch his campaign got off to a sorry start.

He was frustrated at every turn by all sorts of obstacles, including these:

★ In conferring with the royal Governors he learned that they refused to pool their money and supplies for his use. They had a common fund for gifts for the Indians, he was told, but that was all.

★ To carry his supplies and artillery, he demanded scores of wagons, horses, and drivers. The best the colonists could do was supply twenty-five wagons, most of them in broken-down condition.

★ He was told that the best road to Wills Creek (renamed Fort Cumberland) was through Maryland, but when he got to Frederick, Maryland, he learned there was no road.

★ Some of the supplies of food accumulated for him were already rotting.

★ In Pennsylvania, his Quartermaster General,

Sir John St. Clair, became so infuriated with local residents because of their lack of cooperation that he threatened to kill their cattle, burn their homes, and treat them "like a parcel of traitors."

Later, in Frederick, General Braddock also exploded in rage. "This expedition is over," he bellowed. "Be damned to the colonists. Let the French take them!"

Alarmed by these and other tirades, a soft-spoken, forty-nine-year-old Pennsylvanian rushed to Frederick and arrived just in time to prevent Braddock from aborting the campaign. His name was Benjamin Franklin.

"Mr. Franklin," Braddock said when they met, "you have the reputation of being able to get things done."

"I try," Franklin said modestly.

"If I'm to go on, I need one hundred and fifty wagons and fifteen hundred horses," Braddock said. "Can you get them for me?"

"It may be expensive," Franklin said.

"How expensive?"

"A wagon, four horses and a driver would come to, say, fifteen shillings a day. Horses alone and unattended, about two shillings a day."

"Agreed!" Braddock barked, even though he considered the prices outrageous. "But they need to be delivered to Fort Cumberland by May 10."

"I'll see what we can do," Franklin said.

$\mathcal{C}\mathcal{L} \mathbf{B}$y prior agreement, Braddock's newly appointed aide-de-camp was to meet the General in Frederick in early May.

In the meantime, Washington decided to take his brother Jack with him to visit his property at Bullskin Creek and go from there to Frederick.

On April 30, several days after reaching Bullskin Creek, he sent a brief letter to Sally Fairfax, saying he would continue to write her at "every opportunity."

"It will be needless to expatiate on the pleasures that communication of this kind will afford me," he added, "as . . . a correspondence with my friends is the greatest satisfaction I expect to enjoy in the course of this campaign, and that none of my friends are able to convey more real delight than you can to whom I stand indebted for so many obligations."

Despite the fact that she was married, Sally eventually responded favorably to this appeal, and the two continued to correspond, although secretly and in guarded terms.

$\mathcal{C}\mathcal{L} \mathbf{I}$t was early May by the time Braddock, with Washington at his side, resolutely began to move his army westward toward Fort Duquesne.

Despite grandiose plans and expectations of a swift and decisive victory over the French, however, his glittering, polished troops went forward far too slowly. Often, in fact, the troops became hopelessly bogged down.

"It's the cursed Colonials who are hampering our advance," he roared to anyone who would listen. "The contractors we have been forced to deal with are hostile, inefficient, and dishonest!"

In a letter of complaint to the Governor of Maryland, he said, "I have met with nothing but lies and villainy!"

Only Benjamin Franklin, he added, lived up to the terms of his contract with the Army by supplying the one hundred and fifty wagons and horses he requested and desperately needed.

But lack of supplies and Colonial cooperation were only part of Braddock's difficulties.

Instead of using pack animals to cross the forbidding Alleghenies, as Washington had suggested, Braddock insisted that his men construct a wide, graded road over the mountains; mountains that he had never seen and about which he knew very little.

The first range that Braddock's men encountered was an almost perpendicular elevation of some 3,000 feet, all of it rock!

And ahead lay Laurel Hill with a height of 2,400 feet, and beyond that Chestnut Ridge at 2,200 feet.

Despite the efforts of three hundred grunting, cursing, growling men, it took three days to conquer the first ridge. In the process, several wagons were shattered, three completely destroyed and their teams killed.

Still, Braddock pressed on.

But the heavy loads and the rugged terrain rapidly weakened both horses and men. On June 16, the stubborn Englishman finally faced reality and sent his aides scurrying along the line of march to pass a one-word order: "Halt!"

In the previous ten days, the army had covered only twenty-two miles. At that pace, Braddock knew he could never reach Duquesne before the French learned he was coming and called in reinforcements. He also realized that if he didn't somehow change his plans, all would be lost.

Summoning Washington to his tent, he told the young Virginian of his concerns. Then he asked bluntly, "What do you suggest?"

"Well, sir, I would suggest two things. First, I would send a lightly equipped column forward with packhorses as soon as possible. We're in the midst of a drought, and the rivers are low. That means the French will have difficulty coming down from the north with more men, arms, and supplies.

"I would also lighten the wagons and have them follow the advance force at a safe distance."

Braddock made no comment before dismiss-

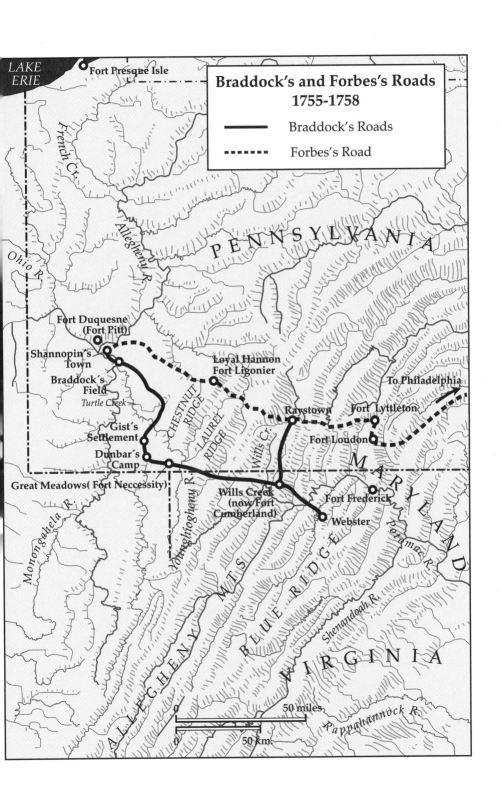

Braddock's and Forbes's Roads
1755-1758

————— Braddock's Roads

- - - - - - Forbes's Road

LAKE ERIE

Fort Presque Isle

French Cr.

Allegheny R.

Ohio R.

PENNSYLVANIA

Fort Duquesne (Fort Pitt)

Shannopin's Town

Braddock's Field

Turtle Creek

Loyal Hannon Fort Ligonier

To Philadelphia

Gist's Settlement

CHESTNUT RIDGE

LAUREL RIDGE

Raystown

Fort Lyttleton

Dunbar's Camp

Wills Cr.

Fort Loudon

Great Meadows(Fort Neccessity)

MARYLAND

Monongahela R.

Youghiogheny R.

Wills Creek (now Fort Cumberland)

Fort Frederick

Webster

ALLEGHENY MTS.

BLUE RIDGE

Potomac R.

Shenandoah R.

VIRGINIA

Rappahannock R.

50 miles

0

50 km

ing his aide. But the next day, Washington was pleased to see his plan put in motion.

Unfortunately, he and scores of others became ill with the "bloody flux," or dysentery. When all was in readiness two days later, Braddock's orders rang down the lines. Sluggishly, but at a quicker pace than before, the army resumed its march.

It did so without Washington. The young soldier was terribly weak and in great pain. He was also deeply disappointed, convinced that any engagement with the enemy would be over by the time he recovered.

He was wrong.

After lying on his back for a week, Washington was again able to travel. This time, however, it was aboard a cart; his saddle horse and a packhorse were tied to the tailgate and trotted behind.

Although in considerable pain as he sat in the bouncing, swaying wagon, Washington hurried his team along the trail, for General Braddock was now some twenty-five miles ahead. As he did so, he quickly passed several familiar landmarks: Fort Necessity, Jumonville's camp, and Christopher Gist's settlement.

He finally reached Braddock twelve miles southeast of Fort Duquesne. The date was July 8.

And just as he arrived, the General called a council of war.

Braddock minced no words as the officers gathered around him.

"When next we move, we will capture Duquesne, the objective that will enable us to regain control of the Ohio Valley," he said with utmost confidence.

The officers applauded and cheered. Braddock signaled for silence.

"It's time now to make our final plans," he said.

The first called on to speak were two Indian scouts who had gone ahead of the column early that day. Both had little to report, but one proudly displayed the scalp of a French officer he said he killed near the fort.

Christopher Gist, Washington's old friend and guide, had also scouted ahead for Braddock's troops.

"I almost lost my own scalp when I came upon two French Indians east of the fort," he said. "They were only a few feet away, but the woods were so thick they couldn't see me."

"And you escaped by a hair," Washington called out, bringing a laugh from the relaxed, confident officers.

"Yes," Gist said, joining in the laughter. "There was also some smoke between here and the fort and I saw two boats on the river. No other activity, though."

Now, St. Clair suggested that Braddock send a force to the fort under cover of darkness to investigate while most of the French were asleep.

This was voted down.

"No one listens to me," St. Clair grumbled.

A second proposal was to wait until the troops and wagon train trailing Braddock under command of Colonel Thomas Dunbar could catch up.

This too was voted down because it would take Dunbar one or two days to reach the main army, and too much food would be consumed.

Next, the senior engineer, Patrick MacKellar, described the lay of the land ahead with the aid of a crude map fastened to a tree.

After digesting MacKellar's report, it was agreed that the principal line of march would be between the Monongahela on the left and Turtle Creek, a stream running parallel on the right. This was a wide swath of open land, bordered by woods on either side, called "the Narrows."

It was also agreed, however, that because of difficult terrain directly ahead, the army would cross the Monongahela after about two miles, follow it for a few more miles, then cross back to the right bank. From that point on, Braddock was assured, there was an easy, straight path to the French fort.

This, then, was the main thrust of the battle plan. When the details were filled in — such as who would be in the vanguard and rear guard, and the placement of various field pieces in the line — the plan satisfied Braddock and his senior officers.

The British experience in Europe, against opponents who fought as they did, told them all would go well.

Only Washington and the Virginians knew what might be expected. Obviously, their voices, even if raised, would never have been heard.

At 2 A.M. on July 9, Braddock's disciplined troops came quickly alive.

Washington, his fever gone, tied a cushion to his saddle, mounted, and went to his post at the General's side.

Following the plan hatched the night before, the various segments of the army methodically moved into their assigned places.

By 8 A.M., with Lieutenant Colonel Thomas Gage in the lead, some fifteen hundred men — plus horses, wagons, artillery, and cattle — were on the move in a narrow line that stretched through the Narrows for about two thousand yards.

The river crossings, considered the most vulnerable to attack, were cleared without incident and the officers began congratulating themselves.

At 2 o'clock that afternoon, however, a volley of gunshots was heard from the front.

Braddock, riding at midpoint in the column, ordered a halt. Just as he was about to send Washington to investigate, Harry Gordon, an engineer who had been with the advance party, ran his horse directly to the General and slid the animal to a halt.

"Excellency, we ran into a band of some three hundred Indians and French!" he shouted excitedly. "They were stripped to the waist and moving in our direction. When they saw us, they disappeared into the woods on either side of the column, screamed like bloody murder, and opened fire."

"Any casualties?" Braddock asked.

"Many," was the grim response.

Before Braddock could ask another question, the bloodcurdling whoops of Indians and the firing on both sides of the column moved swiftly closer.

The British tried to answer, but could find no one to shoot at. In less than an hour, there was chaos.

The troops in front, terrified by the yells of Indians they couldn't see, panicked and scrambled to the rear. Those on the flanks also tried to retreat but were hampered by the terrified men, the horses, and the equipment crushed between and behind.

General Braddock's army suffered one of the worst defeats in military history as it attempted to take Fort Duquesne in July of 1755.

Most of the mounted officers who tried to rally their men were easy targets and soon were on the ground—wounded, dead, or dying.

From the front, the right, and the left, the firing from the hidden Indians and French not only continued but intensified.

Washington begged Braddock to allow him to take troops up a hill on the right and into the woods where they could make a stand. At first, the bewildered General refused. After conditions worsened, he relented. But it was too late.

In trying to rally the troops, Washington had two horses shot from under him. One bullet went through his hat, three others slit his coat.

Braddock finally ordered a withdrawal. As he did, a bullet crashed through his arm and lodged in his lung. By now, hundreds of British were running pell-mell to the rear.

Still alive as the sun went down, Braddock realized that someone had to ride to Dunbar and bring him forward to rescue what was left of his army. He turned to Washington.

"You're the only one who knows the trail well enough to stay on it in the dark," Braddock said. "Will you go and bring Dunbar up?"

"I will try, Excellency," Washington said.

By now Washington had been in the saddle for more than twelve hours. Though weak from his illness and bone-weary from the rigors of the day, he threaded his horse through the fleeing

men, many of whom were wounded and also dying, and set out on his mission; a mission he was
determined to accomplish.

Clinging weakly to his saddle on
a horse that could hardly stand, Washington
reached Dunbar's camp just before noon on the
morning of July 10.

Three days later, he and Dunbar met General
Braddock and the retreating army. Braddock and
three of his staff officers, including Robert Orme,
his favorite, were being carried eastward on horse
litters.

Near Great Meadows, Braddock, weakened by
a loss of blood, called a halt and summoned Dunbar and Orme to his side.

After telling Dunbar to take command, he
turned to Orme.

"I want you to report what happened to those
at home," he said. "And say nothing could equal
the gallantry and good conduct of the officers nor
the bad behavior of the men."

A few hours later, he died.

As the only staff member on his feet, it fell
to Washington to bury Braddock and conduct the
service. Knowing the habits of warring Indians,
Washington chose a spot in the road at the head
of the column and had a grave dug.

After Braddock's body was slipped into it and covered, he had the entire column—horses, wagons, and booted soldiers—pass over the freshly turned earth.

"Why was that necessary?" Dunbar asked.

"If the French Indians know where the General is buried they may very well dig up the body and mutilate it," he answered.

The body was never found.

Of the almost fifteen hundred men who marched against Duquesne, less than five hundred survived. The shattered army now faced the ordeal of again crossing the mountains and returning to the safety of Fort Cumberland.

It was a long, torturous retreat. Many men died along the way. When Washington finally reached Fort Cumberland, his appearance created a sensation.

"We had a report that you were dead!" the commanding officer explained.

"Obviously, I'm not," a weary Washington responded. "Was this report forwarded to Williamsburg?"

"Of course," came the reply.

Washington quickly wrote friends and family, assuring them that he was alive and recovering from the ordeal of the campaign.

To his brother Jack, he said he was ". . . in the land of the living by the miraculous care of Providence that protected me beyond all human expectation."

He wrote a similar letter to his mother and thoughtfully asked her to tell a woman in her neighborhood that her son had escaped the debacle with a minor wound to one of his feet.

But a letter to Dinwiddie took a different direction. "I tremble at the consequences that this defeat may have on our back settlers, who I suppose will leave their habitations unless there are proper measures taken for their security."

In this he was correct. As soon as word of Braddock's defeat spread, scores of frontier families packed their belongings and fled eastward.

Many of those who stayed, however, were massacred by marauding French Indians. And in August, when Colonel Dunbar took what remained of the British regulars and three companies of Virginia independents into "winter" quarters in Philadelphia, the frontier was left completely unprotected.

A panicky General Assembly promptly voted to use forty thousand pounds for the defense of the colony. But again the question was raised: Who would lead the twelve hundred men to be recruited to protect the frontier?

On August 13, 1755, Washington—whose service to the Crown ended with Braddock's death and ignoble defeat at Duquesne—accepted appointment as "Commander in Chief" of all Virginia forces.

He was twenty-three and one-half years old.

For almost three years, Washington attempted to defend against the incursions of the French and their Indians. He did so by building a string of forts from the borders of Maryland to the Carolinas.

His efforts were far from successful, and he blamed it on the weakness of the recruiting laws, the lack of money and provisions, and the failure of the government to enlist the aid of friendly Indians.

Late in July 1757, he was again stricken with the "bloody flux." Even though he grew weaker day by day, he refused to give up his duties on the frontier. Four months later, fever and chest pains made him turn to Dr. James Craik, a new, young regimental surgeon, for help.

"I'd advise bloodletting," Dr. Craik said after examining Washington.

"Bloodletting?" Washington asked, not believing he heard correctly.

"Yes. Your blood is probably contaminated. We'll drain some and the body will manufacture new blood. It's a method that's been used since early Roman times."

Though it was done during the time he was stricken with the "bloody flux," Washington showed his approval of this portrait by putting his signature on it.

"How do you do it?"

Warming to the subject, Dr. Craik said, "At first, doctors used sharp thorns, roots, fish teeth, and even sharpened stones to cut a vein and let the blood out. I use a phlebotome, or lancet."

Washington, desperate for help, agreed to the procedure. Dr. Craik gave him a stick to hold in his right hand, tied a tourniquet above his right bicep, punctured a vein in his elbow, and drained a quart of blood from his body.

Despite the treatment Washington's condition did not improve. In fact, he could hardly walk and was forced to turn over his command to Captain Robert Stewart and return home.

During the winter months, he went from doctor to doctor trying to find a cure for his ailment, but to no avail. He became convinced that he was suffering from the disease that killed his brother Lawrence.

In January he tried to ride to Williamsburg to consult Dr. John Amson, who was said to have extensive experience with the flux. He was so weak, however, that he had to turn back to Mount Vernon.

From time to time during January and February he was nursed by Sally Fairfax. By March he was considerably improved. Still, he was concerned enough to attempt another trip to the doctor in Williamsburg.

In great pain, he rode slowly southward, stopping frequently to rest at the homes of friends and even at Ferry Farm, where his mother again nagged at him to "once and for all get out of the Army."

As he neared Williamsburg, he visited Major Richard Chamberlayne, an old army friend. Washington planned to have only the midday meal with Chamberlayne and his wife.

The Chamberlaynes, he soon learned, had overnight visitors, a pretty widow and two small children.

The widow's name was Martha Dandridge Custis.

Washington and Mrs. Custis were not strangers. They had met occasionally at Virginia's most prestigious social events, the twice-yearly Assembly Balls in Williamsburg.

At the time, of course, she was still married to Daniel Parke Custis, whom she had married when she was seventeen, even though he was twenty years older.

Their meeting at the Chamberlaynes, however, was the first time that she and Washington spent any length of time in each other's company. During the visit, which included an overnight stay and a leisurely breakfast the next morning, they talked at length about many things.

At the time of her engagement to George Washington, Martha Dandridge Custis was a widow in her mid-twenties with two small children.

Washington also played enthusiastically with four-year-old Jacky and his sister, two-year-old Patsy. Before he left the next morning, to the squealing delight of the children, he put them both on his horse and led the horse around the Chamberlaynes' circular driveway several times.

Obviously, Virginia's most eligible bachelor and one of the Colony's richest women were strongly attracted to each other.

When the good-byes to the Chamberlaynes and the Custis family were said and Washington mounted his horse to leave for Williamsburg, Martha Custis had one last comment:

"Why don't you stop at my home on your way back, Colonel? The children and I would love to see you again."

"That's an invitation I can hardly refuse," Washington said.

Tipping his hat, he rode off.

Dr. Amson had encouraging news.

"You do not have tuberculosis," he told Washington. "And the flux has run its course. You'll be just fine if you take care of yourself and watch your diet."

Washington was, of course, elated. Staying on in Williamsburg, he visited members of the Assembly and the new Governor.

Not long afterward, he headed for the Custis plantation. Admired locally for its six chimneys, the White House, as it was known, was located not far from the Chamberlaynes on the banks of the Pamunkey River.

Washington had a long and pleasant visit and, as before, played with the children until, exhausted, they were sent off to bed.

Sometime during that visit, Washington and Mrs. Custis apparently became engaged. Both—independently—almost immediately ordered new finery from London.

In Washington's letter to a clothier he requested "as much of the best superfine blue cotton velvet as will make a coat, waistcoat and breeches for a tall man, with fine silk buttons to suit it . . . six pairs of the neatest shoes and six pairs of gloves . . . ."

These items, he wrote, were to be put aboard the first vessel to leave England for any port in Virginia.

Martha's order asked for "one genteel suit of clothes for myself to be grave, but not to be extravagent and not to be mornning." Suitable as a wedding dress, in other words.

For local folk—including the Fairfaxes—Washington's intentions became clear when he quickly launched plans to rebuild Mount Vernon. Based on his own design, the roof was to be raised and a second story added to what was previously a one-and-a-half-story farmhouse.

When he left Mount Vernon to rejoin his troops, he was assured that George William Fairfax would supervise the construction work. As a result, there's little doubt that his wife, Sally, was well informed of Washington's matrimonial plans.

But before there could be a wedding, Washington was to face another harrowing adventure. And some second thoughts.

As spring rolled into summer, William Pitt was named Prime Minister of England. He immediately announced that the Crown would launch a three-pronged attack to dislodge the French from the North American continent.

As part of this plan, General John Forbes was to be in command of the force of regulars and colonists who would again attempt to cross the rugged Allegheny Mountains and to capture Fort Duquesne.

While waiting for Forbes to appear, Washington exchanged letters with Sally Fairfax. They always burned their letters, but this revealing letter has survived.

Camp at Fort Cumberland 12th Sept.r 1758–
Dear Madam,
Yesterday I was honourd with your short, but very agreeable favour of the first Inst.t —

how joyfully I catch at the happy occasion of renewing a Corrispondance which I feard was disrelished on your part, I leave to time, that never failing Expositor of all things—and to a Monitor equally as faithful in my own Breast to Testifie.—In silence I now express my joy . . . .

If you allow that any honour can be derivd from my opposition to our present System of management you destroy the merit of it entirely in me by attributing my anxiety to the annimating prospect of possessing Mrs. Custis.—When—I need not name it.—guess yourself.—Should not my own Honour and Country's welfare be the excitement? Tis true, I profess myself a Votary of Love—I acknowledge that a Lady is in the Case—and I further confess, that this Lady is known to you.—Yes Madam as well as she is to one who is too sensible of her Charms to deny the Power, whose Influence he feels and must ever Submit to. I feel the force of her amiable beauties in the recollection of a thousand tender passages that I could wish to obliterate, till I am bid to revive them.—but experience alas! sadly reminds me how Impossible this is.—and evinces an Opinion which I have long entertained, that there is a Destiny, which has the Sovereign controul of our Actions—not to be resisted by the strongest efforts of Human Nature.

You have drawn me my dear Madam, or rather I have drawn myself, into an honest confession of a Simple Fact—misconstrue

Although he was engaged to Martha, Washington kept up his correspondence with Sally Fairfax, his longtime friend and unrequited love.

not my meaning—'tis obvious—doubt [it] not, nor expose it,—the World has no business to know the object of my Love,—declared in this manner to-you when I want to conceal it . . . .

I cannot expect to hear from my Friends more than this once, before the Fate of the Expedition will some how or other be determined, I therefore beg to know when you set out for Hampton, & when you expect to Return to Belvoir again . . . .

Several readings of this deliberately confusing letter make several things clear:

* ★ Sally knew about the forthcoming wedding to Martha.
* ★ Washington had been in love with Sally for a long time.
* ★ He felt it was no one else's business.
* ★ He recognized that nothing could be done about the situation.
* ★ He still would like to hear from her.

Soon, however, he had other, more critical matters to worry about.

To Washington's dismay and anger, General John Forbes, the new British commander, decided to land his army in Philadelphia and follow a route to Raystown (now Bedford, Pennsylvania) where he would establish a base of operations. From there, he planned to cut a new road over the Alleghenies.

"It would be much easier and save a great deal of time," Washington argued, "to go southwestward to Fort Cumberland and pick up Braddock's road."

Forbes and his top officers, however, were adamant about taking a direct route to Duquesne. On reaching Raystown, Forbes brought his army to a halt to await the outcome of peace negotiations then going on between British ambassadors and various Indian tribes, including many of those who had sided with the French.

On October 27, Forbes learned that a peace treaty had been signed. Despite this late date, he led a force of seven thousand regulars and colonials, an army three times larger than Braddock's, in slow stages over the mountains. This time, Washington was in command of two regiments of colonials.

On the far side of Laurel Ridge, at a place called Loyal Hannon, Forbes set up another base.

Shortly after the army's arrival, scouts reported a group of French nearby.

Forbes, so ill from the flux he had to be carried in a horse litter, called Washington to his tent.

"Take five hundred men and see if you can find them," he said. "George Mercer will follow with another five hundred. Perhaps you can trap the French between you and destroy them."

Washington set out, and in the late afternoon three miles from Loyal Hannon, he found a party of French and Indians around a campfire. There was an exchange of fire. Several of the enemy were killed or wounded. While some escaped, three prisoners were captured.

As Washington and his men prepared to return to the base, a large force approached in the darkness and opened fire. Washington's group promptly responded.

"Cease fire!" Washington bellowed, knocking up muskets with his sword. "Cease fire! It's Mercer!"

It was too late. One officer and thirteen soldiers were killed, and twenty-six were wounded.

Later, the prisoners were interrogated separately. They told the same story: Duquesne was only lightly defended.

"If they're telling the truth," Forbes said late that night at a council, "this might be our chance. If, on the other hand, they're not—and considering the lateness of the season—perhaps we'd better wait another year."

The vote was unanimous: Move on to Duquesne!

In the interest of speed, Forbes put twenty-five hundred of the strongest men into three brigades, one of which was under Washington's command.

Technically, this made him a Brigadier. He was pleased and fell to his assigned task with vigor, clearing a road toward Duquesne.

For ten days, the three brigades moved

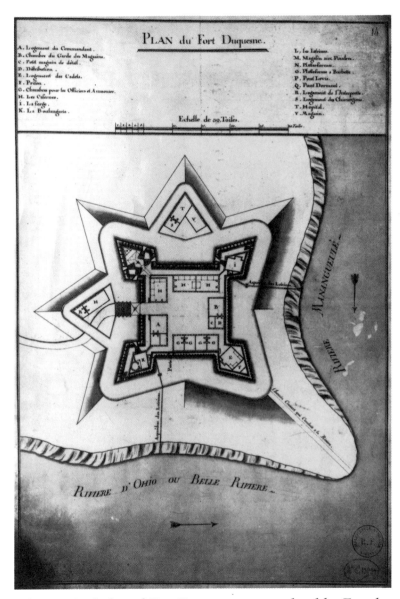

This original plan of Fort Duquesne was rendered by French engineers. The Allegheny River is labeled the Ohio, in accordance with French usage.

quickly but cautiously forward, taking every precaution against the kind of disaster that befell Braddock.

Soldiers were warned not to fire a musket without an order from an officer. And each night the men slept on their guns and were ordered not to speak.

Early on the morning of November 19, Washington's scouts reported finding tracks of a large party not far ahead. "But they're heading away from us!" the officer in charge said.

The three brigades hurried ahead. On the evening of November 24, an Indian scout reported that he had come close to the fort and saw a large cloud of smoke. "Smoke?" Washington fairly shouted. "Smoke?"

A second scout rushed in. "The fort is on fire!" he cried. Duquesne, abandoned by the French, fell on the same day without a shot being fired.

As soon as he heard that Duquesne had been taken, Forbes ordered Washington to post a garrison at the ruined fort, then ride to Williamsburg and persuade Virginia's new Governor, Francis Fauquier, to provide for the troops. He then left for Philadelphia, where he died a few weeks later.

By the time Washington returned to civilization, it was almost Christmas. He had not seen
his bride-to-be in six months, and he was discour-
aged to learn that Mount Vernon was not yet
ready to receive her.

Nevertheless, he and Martha went ahead with
their plans: He would go on to Williamsburg, kiss
the new Governor's hand, wind up his Army affairs and be back in time for the wedding.

Washington married Martha Custis on January 6, 1759. They were both twenty-seven.

The ceremony, attended by Martha's children,
the Governor, and a small group of relatives and
friends, took place at the White House, which
was to be their home until work was completed
on Mount Vernon in the spring.

The bride wore a dress of yellow brocade that
was open at the front over a white petticoat, and
high-heeled, lilac slippers embroidered in silver
and gold. Her hair was powdered, the fashion of
the day, and adorned with a strand of pearls.

The groom was said to have worn his dress
uniform of buff and blue.

Since Washington had been elected to the
House of Burgesses while he was at the front, the
happy couple went to Williamsburg in February
for the first session of the Assembly and the Assembly Ball.

When Washington took his seat, his fellow
Burgesses applauded vigorously. Then one of

them rose and said, "Be it noted that this body has voted Colonel Washington our thanks for his faithful services to His Majesty and this Colony, and for his brave and steady behavior from the first encroachments and hostilities of the French

In their wedding finery ordered from England, George Washington and Martha Dandridge Custis were married on January 6, 1759.

and their Indians, to his resignation after the happy reduction of Fort Duquesne."

Blushing, Washington rose and bowed to more applause. "Thank you," he said, nodding to all those seated about him. "Thank you."

It was, of course, a fitting ending to a hazardous, painful struggle begun five-and-a-half years
earlier when he set out to deliver the King's message to the French during the winter months of
1753.

But it was only the beginning of a long, loving
marriage and the greatest political and military
career in American history.

Epilogue

It is not too difficult to learn from the preceding account who and what shaped Washington's extraordinary career. We know that even as a teenager he had a burning ambition to educate and make something of himself; notably by his efforts to emulate his brother Lawrence.

In his first trip to the Ohio at the bidding of Governor Dinwiddie, he successfully carried out a dangerous, almost impossible mission without any training, background, or leadership.

From then on, despite many mistakes and setbacks, he showed he was tenacious, brave, resourceful, hard-working, and—even under the worst of conditions—could remain focused on his objectives.

There is, however, something else to remember about Washington, as can be seen in two letters written by his subordinates during and after the Forbes campaign.

In the first letter Robert Munford told a friend: "Our Colonel is an example of fortitude in either danger or hardship, and by his easy, polite behavior, has gained not only the regard but the affection of both his officers and soldiers."

The second letter was signed by twenty-seven of Washington's officers and sent to him after he left the Army.

It reads as follows:

In our earliest infancy, you took us under your tuition, trained us up in the practice of that discipline which alone can constitute good troops, from the punctual observance of which you never suffered the least deviation.

Your steady adherence to impartial justice, your quick discernment and invariable regard to merit, wisely intended to inculcate those genuine sentiments of true honor and passion for glory, from which the great military achievements have been derived, first heightened our natural emulation and our desire to excel. How much we improved by those regulations and your own example, with what cheerfulness we have encountered the several toils, especially while under your particular direction, we submit to yourself, and flatter ourselves that we have in great measure answered your expectations.

In you we place the most implicit confidence. Your presence only will cause a steady firmness and vigor to actuate in every breast, despising the greatest dangers and thinking light of toils and hardships, while led on by the man we know and love.

Clearly, Washington demonstrated from the out-set of his military career that he had a rare abil-ity: the ability to lead and have others follow.

It was this ability that ultimately gave America its greatest hero.

Important Dates
1732–1759

1732	*February 22*	George Washington born at Wakefield, Westmoreland County, Virginia
1743	*April 12*	Death of father, Augustine Washington
1748	*March–April*	Embarked on surveying party across Blue Ridge with Lord Fairfax
1749	*July 20*	Appointed surveyor of Culpeper County, Virginia
1751	*September 28*	Traveled to Barbados with half brother, Lawrence Washington
1752	*July 26*	Death of Lawrence Washington
	November 6	Appointed Major in Virginia militia

1753	*October–* *January 1754*	Sent by Governor Dinwiddie to deliver ultimatum to French (Fort Le Boeuf)
1754	*March–October*	Lieutenant Colonel of militia in frontier campaign
	July 4	Surrenders Fort Neces- sity to French
1755	*April–July*	Aide-de-camp to General Braddock
	August 14	Appointed Commander in Chief of all Virginia forces, responsible for frontier defense
1758	*June–November*	Took part in Forbes expedition against Fort Duquesne
	July 24	Elected to the House of Burgesses of Virginia
1759	*January 6*	Married Martha Dandridge Custis

About the Author

John Rosenburg has had a long, interesting writing career. He was a general correspondent for the United Press during World War II, he wrote the bestseller *The Story of Baseball,* and has most recently focused his writing on historical topics for young people. His first book for the Millbrook Press, *William Parker: Rebel Without Rights,* tells the fascinating story of a fugitive slave and the little-known uprising he took part in, which touched off the largest treason trial in United States history and helped set the stage for the Civil War.

John Rosenburg lives in a suburb of Philadelphia with his wife, Rosemarie.